Encounters with China

Encounters with China

Merchants, Missionaries and Mandarins

TREA WILTSHIRE

FormAsia

Encounters with China
Merchants, Missionaries and Mandarins

Published 1995
ISBN: 962-7283-14-2
© FormAsia Books Limited
Text copyright FormAsia Books Limited
Printed in Hong Kong

Registered Address:
Coopers & Lybrand
10th Floor, Caroline Centre,
28, Yun Ping Road,
Causeway Bay, Hong Kong

Written by Trea Wiltshire
Edited by Judy Bonavia
Proofread by Geraldine Moor
Designed by Lilian Tang Design Limited
Colour separations by Lau Wing Chung
Printed by Yu Luen Offset Printing FTY. Limited

CONTENTS

THE LION AND THE DRAGON

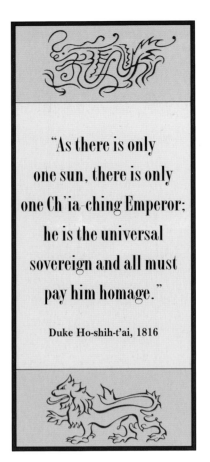

IN THE 19TH CENTURY, AN INCREDIBLE ENCOUNTER TOOK PLACE BETWEEN TWO OF THE greatest empires the world has ever known: the Middle Kingdom of Manchu China and Queen Victoria's small sceptred isle.

Observers from both empires relished portraying the symbolic struggle between two legendary creatures: the Dragon and the Lion. They also delighted in contrasting the expansive empire of the proud Dragon with the Lion's diminutive island kingdom — a kingdom that clearly would contain neither its ambition, nor its appetite for glory.

In that century, China's territory spanned millions of square miles that swept from the northern steppes of Mongolia, through deserts and mist-wreathed mountains, to the rainforests of its southern provinces. And its power extended even beyond those frontiers. It claimed suzerainty over a crescent of vassal nations — stretching from Korea to Turkestan — that annually paid tribute to Peking and were permitted to feast at the table of the Chinese Emperor, the Son of Heaven.

Little wonder the Emperor considered that his mantle of authority extended over "everything under heaven". Little wonder that his subjects believed that he ruled with the Mandate of Heaven, and that China — the Middle Kingdom — was so called because it was closer to heaven than to earth.

Those who lived beyond the empire's charmed circle were thus branded "barbarian", and their arrival on Chinese shores was viewed with a distaste barely disguised by Confucian tolerance.

By the 19th century, when the first major trading and military encounters occurred between China and the West, the Middle Kingdom had become obsessed with preserving, in isolation, all that it possessed: its gilded palaces and pleasure gardens; its treasures that foreign merchants so admired.

Whereas earlier dynasties had sent fleets of imperial junks across the China Seas to trade and gather tribute, Manchu China had become suspicious of the world of challenge and change unfolding beyond its borders. Rumours of distant revolution — of kings being unceremoniously beheaded by ragged revolutionaries — had alarmed the mandarins and princes. As they dined on delicacies, cosseted by concubines, they appreciated that only high walls separated them from a similar hungry peasantry.

So they resisted foreign influence and restricted foreign trading to a brief winter season in the southern city port of Canton, far from Peking's world of privilege. Thus they remained ignorant of the advancing forces that would bring to China new ideas and technology — and plant the seeds of revolution that would bring down

The Empress Dowager Tz'u-hsi.

the Manchu House of Ch'ing, the last dynasty to rule China.

Certainly those in power knew little of Britain, the distant island empire that was outpacing its rivals — Portugal, Holland and France. Britain's naval and military power, allied to its mercantile might, had been quick to exploit the weaknesses of India's Mogul Empire to establish the British Raj in India. It seemed almost inevitable to imperial power brokers that the pattern would ultimately be repeated in China.

The world's first industrial power had factories hungry for raw materials and merchants eager for untapped markets. With the Chinese empire weakened by famine and flood, rebellion and corruption, the time seemed right for an assault on what had always been an irresistible prize.

The territorial "jewels" already mounted in Britain's imperial crown merely served to whet its appetite for more — not only for the glory of conquest, but for the heady allure of landscapes far from the strictures of Victorian society. For the East moved to a different pulse, was flooded with an intensity of colour that was breathtaking.

When in time the battle lines were drawn between the two great empires, it was clear that the contest would be worth watching — for both shared a love of spectacle.

When the Empress Dowager sallied forth from the imperial palace in Peking, the road that led from the twenty-foot-high walls of the Forbidden City were lined with thousands of mandarins in silken gowns. Cavalrymen, standard bearers and pikemen guarded the route, while musicians and trumpeters sounded her approach. As the imperial entourage passed by, thousands prostrated themselves in the dust — in vast undulations of colour — performing the kowtow that caused such consternation to visiting foreign envoys.

And when Queen Victoria's warships, immaculately decked with flags, moved down some fever-infested waterway to lay claim to a distant corner of the globe, the sight stirred the British conviction that the nation was merely fulfiling its destiny. The rhetoric of imperialism promised enlightenment — commercial, religious, moral and social — for subject nations. "Backwardness" would be jettisoned for the benefits of progress and prosperity. The volley of guns, the Union Jack snapping in the breeze and the warships' tremendous wake that swept up native craft, clustering the muddy shoreline — all added to powerful images of an empire that would extend over a quarter of the earth's surface.

From their respective seats of power, the two empresses regarded one another with interest. Victoria Alexandrina, Empress of India, was intrigued by early photographs of the concubine of the second rank who had risen to become the most powerful woman in China. She heard with astonishment of the Empress Dowager's preference for an elixir of crushed pearls and her passion for English clocks — a dozen of which ticked noisily in her apartments in the Forbidden City.

The Empress Dowager, for her part, looked with scorn at the sombre widow's weeds favoured by the stout, unsmiling English empress. As she donned her silken robes, every inch hand-embroidered, she studied the portrait of the English queen that stood by her bed. "Although I have heard much about Queen Victoria," she pronounced, "still I don't think her life is half as interesting and eventful as mine. Now look at me, I have 400 million people all dependent on my judgement."

Queen Victoria took satisfaction in the notion that her bronze statues now stood in the far-flung outposts of the largest empire known to history. The Empress Dowager no doubt derived equal pleasure from the conviction that Victoria's imperial "jewels" would never include China. For the world's oldest empire might lease its land, might reluctantly grant concessions to the foreign powers, might see itself carved into "spheres of influence", but nothing more. Its ancient pride and spirit saw to that.

The century-long encounter of East and West in China was recorded in part by the world's earliest photographers. The curious eye of the camera preserved the dazzling contrasts of that long-gone era — of silken palanquins and horse-drawn carriages; of elaborately carved blackwood furniture and the chinz of punka-cooled interiors; of the mandarin's silks and the merchant's starched collar — images that would be almost impossible to conceive a century later.

This era of encounter would end in the 20th century, with the declaration of the People's Republic of China in 1949, when the nation's new leaders would bring China back to the sort of isolation the Manchus had dreamed of — back in the early days of the encounter.

Queen Victoria, Empress of India.

THE CHINA TRADE

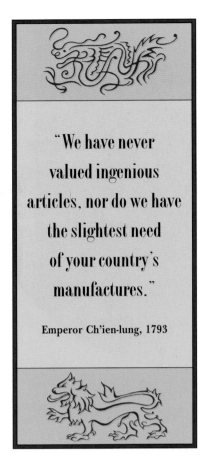

THE ENCOUNTER BEGAN WITH TALK OF TRADE, FOR CHINA'S FABLED WEALTH HAD always excited merchants and mariners across the world. It had lured Columbus across the Atlantic to a new world; Magellan round the Horn to death in the Spice Islands. Eventually every seafaring nation worth its salt would join the race to dominate the rich trade in Eastern spices and to chart a route to the China Seas.

The fleets sailing East borrowed innovations from the empire that attracted them — for the Chinese had employed both multiple masts and sternpost rudders in ocean-going junks as early as the 10th century. They also made good use of two further Chinese inventions — the compass and gunpowder. And having adapted their cannon for naval warfare, fire power would ensure them the upper hand in any skirmishes with Chinese war junks.

Much of the early eastern exploration and enterprise was undertaken by chartered companies with far-reaching powers. The British East India Company had the authority to annex territory, establish trading bases and even engage in hostilities, and by the 17th century it was facing a hostile Dutch counterpart, the Dutch East India Company, determined to maintain its nation's ascendancy in the spice trade.

It was a time of high adventure and untold hazards. Company men from comfortable middle-class homes were dispatched to establish trading posts on far-flung tropical coastlines. Youth was their most vital prerequisite. It helped them to withstand the rigours of the voyage out, and the tropical fevers that could reduce a robust body to fever-wracked delerium in a matter of hours.

These young men of empire ventured into alien cultures with little more than orders against easing the isolation of lonely outposts by fraternizing with locals or seeking solace in an excess of ale. And while they appear to have adopted a cavalier attitude to both imperatives, they rigorously maintained the standards expected of a servant of the British Empire. So they dressed for formal dinners as their mighty East Indiamen ploughed through mountainous seas; made loyal toasts to a distant monarch from the palm-thatched isolation of jungle outposts; and, occasionally had difficulty maintaining the requisite stiff upper lip when beseiged by unfriendly natives or irate Dutch rivals.

Top right: **Regimental guard at Weihaiwei.** *Right:* **The Great Wall, north of the capital.**

As European powers pushed further East, they established
a chain of trading bases that served as stepping stones to the
coast of Cathay. But while China's merchant class was
eager to engage in foreign trade, its mandarin elite was
reluctant to receive anything but respectful tributes
from "barbarian" nations. This aversion was partly
shaped by pride in the Middle Kindom's self-
sufficiency and the belief of scholar officials that
trade was a lowly pursuit. It also had its source in a not
unreasonable fear of invasion. For not even the Great Wall
had succeeded in securing the empire against nomadic
northerners who viewed it as a treasure house worth plundering.
It had proved irresistible to Genghis Khan and his Mongols in the
13th century and to the Manchus who established the ruling Ch'ing dynasty in the 17th century.

Once established, the latter ushered in an era of prosperity that would see Manchu China almost triple
the size of the empire. But expanded frontiers were all the more difficult to police and the alien dynasty was also
aware that anti-Manchu sentiment still simmered — especially in the secret societies of the south where patriots

had entered monasteries rather than wear the Manchu pigtail that symbolized submission.

The troublesome southerners also evinced a distressing desire to engage in trade — and even to emigrate to establish trading bases far from the graves of their ancestors. When anti-Manchu secret societies in the south received support from communities of emigrant Chinese there was a further hardening of official attitudes to trade.

Thus when envoys from European nations sought to extend trade, the Emperor remained adamant: trade with foreigners would remain restricted to the single southern city port of Canton, and to a brief winter trading season.

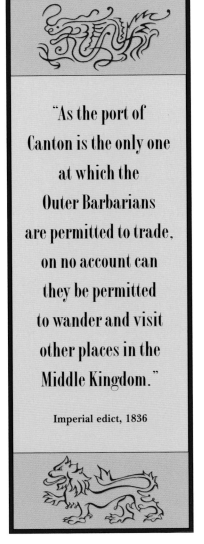

"As the port of Canton is the only one at which the Outer Barbarians are permitted to trade, on no account can they be permitted to wander and visit other places in the Middle Kingdom."

Imperial edict, 1836

As foreign trading ships approached the city port of Canton, they moved between hillsides that reared above the suddenly constricted waters of the Pearl River. Cannons loomed from the forts guarding this southern gateway to China and as ships approached Canton, they came within point-blank range of each battery in turn.

Sailing through the Lion's Gate was initially daunting to foreign fleets. However, they soon appreciated that — as with other aspects of encounter with Manchu China — all was not as it seemed. The forts' cannons were fixed in masonry and a fast-moving frigate with movable cannon could elude them while reducing the forts to rubble.

Each time a British naval vessel forced its way through the Lion's Gate, those in charge of the forts were publicly disgraced, stripped of rank and replaced with a great show of imperial outrage. But the flawed forts were never strengthened and became a symbol — of China's refusal to respond to a changing world, and of the ineffectual chain of command between the Emperor in the far north and his provincial Viceroy in the south.

Despite its restrictions, the ships of many nations took advantage of winter trading in Canton.

The British East India Company, which enjoyed a monopoly on its nation's trade with China until the 1830s, brought raw cotton from Bombay, tins and rattan from Malacca, and novelties such as finely-crafted British clocks and musical snuffboxes. However, Chinese purchases were minimal. Not even the nation's traditional staple — its woollens — excited demand, for in China the rich kept warm with quilted silks and furs while the poor merely added layers of cotton padding to their blue homespun.

When trading ships arrived at Canton, coolies swiftly unloaded their merchandise at waterfront

Foreign "factories" on the opposite shore at Canton.

warehouses, or "factories", where foreign merchants lived and traded. Later their vessels were reloaded with quantities of silk, porcelain and lacquerware.

But tea was the most important, single commodity of the China Trade. It was the Company's most lucrative source of revenue and one which annually netted the British government several million pounds — in fact, half the cost of maintaining the Royal Navy.

China teas were sold as a luxury cure-all that, according to the tea merchants of London's Mincing Lane, effectively countered "gripping of the gut, colds, dropsy and scurvey". Taking tea became a pleasurable ritual, and those who savoured the fragrant brew also enjoyed the images it conjured: of the distant upcountry tea gardens; of tea chests being carried through mountain passes on the backs of long lines of porters; and of their arrival in Canton on graceful riverine junks.

By the beginning of the 19th century, Britain had acquired such a liking for China's tea that it was consuming some twenty million pounds a year. When private merchants assumed control of the trade, once the Company's monopoly ended, they urged their shipyards to produce faster vessels. Thus the slow-moving, armed East Indiamen gave way to the slender elegance of tea clippers in the 1850s.

Able to sail into the monsoon winds, the clippers came to epitomize the romance of the age of sail — and they won the merchant princes not only the best prices at the London tea auctions, but honours in an annual race of tea clippers from the South China Sea to the English Channel.

Those who gathered on the English coast to lay bets on the advancing clippers were also intrigued by the tales of the princely lifestyles sustained by their taste for tea. For while the merchants complained volubly about the restricted conditions in which they lived and worked in Canton, many maintained palatial mansions in England and spacious summer homes in Portuguese Macao, at the mouth of the Pearl River estuary. The latter, settled by the Portuguese since the 16th century, was home to the merchants when they were not trading in Canton.

While their ships awaited the arrival of the annual tea crop, the merchants lived and worked in their Canton "factories" — terraced buildings, with painted shutters and colonnaded façades, that housed British, American, Dutch, Spanish, Swedish, Danish and Parsee merchants.

This small international enclave was all the foreign merchants would know of China during the five-month trading season. Since Canton had been opened to foreign trade in the 17th century, trade had been restricted to a winter season during which the merchants were not permitted to venture beyond the designated area of the factories. The few Chinese permitted to deal with them — a body of monopolistic contractors known as the Hong merchants — were forbidden to teach them Chinese, nor to have any dealings with them beyond what was strictly necessary. No foreign women were permitted to set foot on Chinese soil — and when a few spirited young women visited the factories, they instantly incurred the wrath of the Viceroy of Canton, and had to return to nearby Macao.

Yet the microcosm of China that the merchants saw from their one-thousand-foot strip of Canton

"Flower boats" on the Canton waterfront.

waterfront provided a spectacle that underscored the frustrations of their confinement.

The veranda of the British factory — the largest and best appointed — provided a panorama of slow-moving, single-masted junks, busy sampans, varnished upcountry tea boats, duck boats, brightly-painted floating brothels or "flower boats", lacquered boats owned by mandarins, salt junks, rice boats, barges, lighters and pilot boats, plus the floating homes of fisherfolk who lived and died afloat and whose homes turned the waterfront into a mass of dancing lights at night.

Those who dined at the British factory in Canton clearly relished this spectacle, and the experience of taking their seats at an impeccably dressed table beneath a crystal chandelier. Long-robed Chinese servants stood behind every chair, waiting to replenish a wineglass or produce a platter. As they savoured their Manila cheroots, the merchants could pass the time at billiards, browse through one of the best libraries in the Far East or stroll on the waterfront to watch the never-ending stream of fortune tellers, jugglers and pedlars.

The people of Canton were equally curious to see the Fan-qui or "foreign devils" who wore tight-fitting clothes, ate with strange metal implements, and were red-faced and hirsute.

They had been warned by the mandarins to treat the foreigners with suspicion, so the occupants of the factories were constantly aware of being isolated by a great crush of humanity — that gathered at gates, peered into windows and surrounded them whenever they ventured out.

Sometimes the crowds were friendly, sometimes jeering and — when incited by the mandarins — downright belligerent. On occasions, when the merchants refused to comply with an official edict, the factories were beseiged by stone-throwing mobs and guards with pikes and spears were added to the angry throng. At such times all trade was suspended, Chinese servants were ordered to leave the factories, and a cacophony of gongs resounded through the night.

However, such occasions were rare and generally of the merchants' making — for they had a cavalier attitude to the mandarins' attempts to turn them into compliant servants of the Middle Kingdom. The Hong merchants saw to it that smuggled provisions reached the incarcerated merchants and, when the storm of official fury had blown over, they might arrange a clandestine adventure for the restless foreigners.

Escaping the factories to visit the high-walled mansion of a Hong merchant was a memorable occasion marked by lavish hospitality. A young American employed by Russell and Company, one of the leading American firms in Canton, was clearly entranced by his first glimpse of a Chinese garden with its artificial lakes and pavilions, its camellias and flowering fruit trees. The shy women of the household also caught his eye with their gowns of embroidered plum, pink and pea green silks. He left with memories of "black eyes, splendid eyebrows and teeth of ivory whiteness", and black hair coiled and dressed with silver or gold ornaments.

While the common interest of maximizing profits bound the foreign merchant and his Chinese counterpart, no such empathy existed with the local mandarinate who made a point of having as little to do with the barbarian merchants as possible. In these early trading encounters with China, the mandarin and merchant became arch adversaries. Both were stubborn, unyielding and almost totally ignorant of one another's thinking.

The mandarin rose to high public office within China's bureaucracy by steeping himself in the classics and mastering the skills of calligraphist, painter and poet. Through an exacting examination system, he graduated from gentleman, to scholar, to revered member of the literati, eventually reaching a position of unassailable authority. However, the mandarin's admirable classical education hardly equipped him for the banal day-to-day demands of his office. It surprised no one that he evinced more interest in the sweep of a calligraphy character than in the grubby world of commerce. Or that a great gulf existed between his world and that of most of the Emperor's subjects who toiled to fill the family's rice bowl by whatever means came to hand.

To the foreign merchant, the mandarin epitomized the hypocrisy of Manchu officialdom. At almost every turn he encountered a pervasive corruption. It began as soon as he entered the Lion's Gate and continued on through to the Hong merchants — who were mercilessly "squeezed" by mandarins not above lining their silken pockets from the commerce they affected to disdain.

The merchant took pride in Britain's newly forged industrial strength, and in the naval superiority that had won the nation victory over Napoleon I in 1815. He had watched British power consolidate in India through the early decades of the 19th century. He knew full well that the commercial aggression he showed would eventually be backed by his nation's fire power.

All he had to do was bide his time on the Canton waterfront and enjoy the profits generated not only from teas and silks, but from an illicit commodity smuggled into China from British India.

Chinese ladies, with bound feet and silken robes, seldom ventured beyond their homes.

THE TRADE IN FOREIGN MUD

WHEN, IN THE 18TH CENTURY, THE BRITISH EAST INDIA COMPANY INHERITED POWER FROM THE CRUMBLING Mogul Empire in India, it acquired an important state-controlled source of revenue: Bengal's fields of crimson and white opium poppies. The potent milky-white sap of the *papâver somniferum* would be sold not only to the domestic market that had always been supplied, but to China.

Opium was widely used across the world, for this was an age when the coloured glass carboys that lined apothecary shop shelves held few effective remedies.

Its addictive properties not yet recognized, the drug and its tinctures were available in pharmacies and included in a fifth of all prescriptions. Freely sold in markets in both Europe and America, opium was used in remedies from rheumatism to bronchitis, malaria to cholera. It also offered a "pennyworth of peace" to women who worked long hours in English mills and left their infants in the care of older children.

Turkish and Arab traders originally introduced opium to both India and China. Initially the Chinese ate and drank the drug, but its popularity extended during the 17th century when they began to mix it with tobacco and smoke it. Edicts from the Emperor — the first issued in 1729 — prohibited use of the drug, but had as little effect as earlier edicts against tobacco.

In China, the wealthy indulged in the pleasurable ritual of an opium pipe in well-appointed divans or in their homes. For the poor, opium-induced dreams offered a brief escape from the treadmill of poverty or ease for aching limbs that had laboured too long.

For the East India Company, Bengal's opium solved the dilemma of how to halt the one-way flow of silver bullion used to purchase teas and silks. Chinese merchants had little interest in buying the goods offered by any of the nations trading in Canton. The Americans had been particularly industrious in presenting an array of merchandise from ginseng root gathered from the Appalachian Mountains to sea otter pelts from the Pacific Northwest. But trade remained heavily weighted in China's favour — until opium was offered.

Almost immediately the trade in opium — or "foreign mud" — flourished, and soon it involved most of the traders operating from the factories in Canton.

Whereas Indians ate or drank opium, in China it was mixed with tobacco and smoked.

Chinese merchants in Canton, long frustrated by Peking's opposition to trade, were already engaged in contraband trading. Opium was just another item, but its impact on the Chinese market ensured that it would eventually be the catalyst for the empire's first major military encounter with a Western power.

To avoid jeopardizing its profitable monopoly of the tea trade, the East India Company sold its opium to "country traders" — such as the shrewd Scottish merchants William Jardine, a former Company surgeon, and James Matheson, whose company dominated the

opium trade in Canton. They shipped their chests of opium to the Pearl River, off-loading them at Lintin Island, just visible from their summer homes in Macao.

Chinese officials conveyed imperial edicts prohibiting the sale of opium — and marked in vermilion, "Tremble and Obey!" — while lining their pockets and occasionally orchestrating mock skirmishes involving Chinese men-of-war junks and foreign opium clippers.

On such occasions imperial junks would converge on Lintin once a clipper had discharged its cargo to the "fast crabs" and "scrambling dragon" smuggling boats that carried it to Canton. While the clipper made a show of fleeing the hostile imperial junks, they set off in pursuit — making sure that their angry cannonade did little more than bid the foreign vessel a noisy farewell. Reports of such skirmishes were routinely dispatched to Peking to convince the Emperor of the vigilance of officials.

In 1833, when the East India Company's trade monopoly ended due to pressure from the merchants, firms such as Jardine Matheson and Company began urging the British government to take a stronger stand over the easing of foreign trade restrictions, arguing persuasively that if more Chinese ports were open to trade, the smuggling would cease.

The merchant's complaints about the contemptuous treatment by their Chinese hosts were familiar to the British government, which had earlier initiated official visits to Peking by British envoys. The first such visit occurred in the last decade of the 18th century, more than forty years before the military encounters that became known as the Opium Wars.

*L*ord Macartney, an Irish peer, had been sent to Peking in 1793 to initiate the first doomed diplomatic encounter with Chinese officials. His brief was to persuade the Emperor Ch'ien-lung to lift trade restrictions, to request the residence of an ambassador in Peking, and to convince China that Britain was not a tributary state — but an empire that enjoyed equal status with China.

The envoy travelled in a sixty-four-gun man-of-war and came laden with gifts that filled an entire chamber at the Imperial Palace in Peking. Chandeliers hung from the ceiling and on the marble floor stood an array of gifts that the Irish peer considered "full of ingenuity, utility and beauty". The artistry of finely-crafted clocks contrasted with the technology of scientific instruments that were heralding change in the Western world.

Certainly the Chinese Court clamoured to see the gifts.

The astronomical lenses and other scientific instruments on display were examined with interest, but clearly they did not have the appeal of a dwarf that could stand on the palm of a hand, or a magic pillow that could transport its user to any destination — gifts which a Chinese newspaper had suggested would be among those presented to the Emperor.

However, the key to failure in this first diplomatic encounter was Macartney's firm refusal to prostrate himself before the Emperor in the traditional kowtow.

In a letter to the British sovereign, George III, Ch'ien-lung attributed Macartney's unacceptable request for an ambassador to the same ignorance that prompted his refusal to perform the kowtow required of all obedient vassals.

"I do not forget the lonely remoteness of your island, cut off from the world by intervening wastes of sea. Nor do I overlook your excusable ignorance of the usages of Our Celestial Empire," he chided the British monarch.

By the time Macartney had embarked on the long return journey, he had accepted the bitter reality that his mission — like so many others to Peking — had been viewed as that of a troublesome vassal state bearing tributes.

Hard on the heels of the British came the Dutch whose envoys prostrated themselves — one losing a powdered wig in the process — to both the Emperor and banners bearing his name. All to no avail.

When a second British mission in 1816 failed to gain even an audience with the Emperor, and the appointment of a Superintendent of Trade in Canton failed to ease the restrictions, tempers began to fray.

The Viceroy of Canton saw the appointment of Lord William Napier as Superintendent of Trade in 1833 as flouting the Emperor's instructions that foreigners could communicate only with appointed Hong merchants. He demanded that Napier leave Canton immediately.

"Nations have their laws," thundered the Viceroy. "Even England has its laws; how much more the Celestial Empire! How flaming bright are its great laws and ordinances. More terrible than the awful thunderbolt. Under this whole bright heaven who dares to disobey them?"

For a while after Napier's arrival in Canton there was a standoff. Napier refused to leave, and the Viceroy refused to have anything to do with him. Then the Governor-General signalled the suspension of trade and a blockade — not only of the factories but also the river.

Napier summoned his frigates but they were unable to approach the beseiged factories. Finally he was forced to withdraw to Macao in humiliating circumstances — conveyed on a small boat, with an escort of jeering Chinese soldiers, gongs and firecrackers.

When Napier arrived in Macao the fever he had contracted in the steamy heat of Canton gathered strength. Borne on a litter to his wife and daughters, he died soon after, having failed to open "the wide field of China to British Spirit and Industry". During his time in China he had allied himself to the leading British merchants Jardine and Matheson, and argued, as they did, that diplomacy be replaced by military muscle.

The opium pipe was a pleasurable ritual enjoyed in well-appointed divans or homes.

The merchant princes appreciated that it was only a matter of time before Britain and the other foreign powers resorted to force. What was needed to spark the conflict was an insult or injustice to foreign subjects or foreign property.

Insults had been legion, but it fell to a high-minded mandarin, given to writing lyrical couplets on fans, to provide the "injustice" that would demand a military response.

High Commissioner Lin Tse-hsu was appointed in 1839 to eradicate the illegal traffic in "foreign mud". Unlike other officials, he could not be "bought" and was determined to succeed where others had turned a blind eye or profited handsomely.

When Commissioner Lin issued an order forbidding any foreign merchant from leaving Canton, blockaded the factories and demanded the merchants surrender their stocks of opium, he provided the fuel for much more

than his subsequent burning of twenty thousand chests of opium worth nearly three million pounds.

But his zeal carried him further. He cut off food supplies to British residents in Macao, forcing families to take refuge on the merchant fleet anchored off the nearby island of Hong Kong. Later the factories were attacked. The scenario needed to stir outrage in the House of Commons had been created.

By "menacing the liberty, lives and properties of the Queen's subjects", Lin played into the hands of the hawks of the British Parliament, and diluted the opposition of those, like Gladstone, who condemned the opium trade as "infamous and atrocious".

The resourceful Scot surgeon-turned-smuggler William Jardine had by that time made his fortune and retired to England. As a Member of Parliament, he lent his voice to those who claimed that the opium dens of China were innocuous, and rather more refined than the bawdy gin palaces of London.

As the matter was discussed in Parliament, it was clear that rather more was at stake than the perceived "insult to the flag". The merchants had surrendered their stocks of opium to Lin on the advice of the Superintendent of Trade in Canton. Predictably they demanded compensation — yet how could the government ask the taxpayers for three million pounds to compensate opium smugglers? It was clear they would have to make war, win and demand a war indemnity from which the smugglers could be reimbursed.

In September 1839, when Chinese men-of-war junks tried to prevent British merchants from buying supplies for the families hounded out of Macao, HMS Volage was ordered to open fire. The twenty-eight-gun frigate unleashed the first broadsides of the Opium War in Hong Kong's harbour — and the irresistible rhetoric of empire in the British House of Commons.

Thomas Babington Macaulay, the Secretary of State for War, stirred the pride of his countrymen as he invoked the image of the British flag being planted on the balcony of the New English Factory in Canton, to revive the spirits of the beseiged merchants.

"The place of this country among nations is not so mean that we should trouble ourselves to resist every petty slight, but there is a limit to that forebearance. It was natural that they should look with confidence on the victorious flag which was hoisted," he intoned, "for it reminded them that they belonged to a country which had made the farthest ends of the earth ring with the fame of her exploits in redressing the wrongs of her children..."

As his voice rang through the House, preparations were already afoot for fifteen men-of-war, five armed steamers and four thousand British, Irish and Indian troops to assemble in the South China Sea.

*Left: **Charred remains of the Canton factories and tea stores.***
*Top: **The International Opium Conference in Shanghai in 1909 consolidated opposition to the trade.***

THE OPIUM WAR

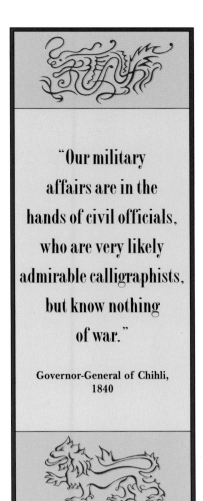

THE OPIUM WAR, THE FIRST MILITARY ENCOUNTER BETWEEN CHINA AND THE WEST, demonstrated both the military superiority of the foreign invaders and their aggressive determination to open the empire to trade. It also graphically illustrated the Middle Kingdom's capacity for self-delusion.

The Emperor had listened to official assurances that the English were "an insignificant and detestable race" whose military might had been highly overrated. He was comforted by assurances that coastal batteries and fire rafts — not to mention monkeys festooned with firecrackers to ignite the frigates' magazines — would create a display of "celestial terror" to annihilate the invaders.

But the reality was at odds with these fanciful tales. Canton fell quickly and, as news of further defeats mounted, the Son of Heaven heard of foreign paddle steamers that could "fly across the water, without wind or tide, with the current or against it", and of how ineffectual fire rafts were against frigates. To successfully launch the latter, the frigate had to be approached at close quarters — an impossible task as it unleashed its broadsides.

First Canton fell, then Amoy, Tinghai, Chinhai, Ningpo and a string of other coastal towns.

While the Ch'ing army fought bravely — and routinely took their own lives and those of their families rather than face defeat — it was clear that its numerical superiority counted for little against the well-equipped and disciplined invading forces.

Britain's scarlet-coated soldiers — the good fighting men who won glory for the empire through the

*Left: **British soldiers at the treaty port of Tientsin and Ch'ing dynasty troops in Peking.***
*Above: **The arsenal at Nanking in the 1870s, built with foreign advice.***

19th century — were also, as Rudyard Kipling observed, "blackguards commanded by gentlemen to do butchers' work with dispatch and efficiency."

When incited by stories of British civilians being paraded through the streets in chains and cages — as had been the fate of those on a merchant vessel that ran aground near Ningpo — they fought fiercely and exacted a terrible toll.

Rape and plunder inevitably attended military victory in the 19th century and was the fate of Ningpo. Even the battle-hardened British commander, Major General Hugh Gough, confessed to being sickened by the carnage and destruction of this first bloody encounter between the empires.

Eventually not even the embellished tales of the Emperor's advisers could disguise the extent of the defeat. It would be a landmark defeat unlike any that had come before; and with it came the first hints of an unravelling

of what had been the seemingly unassailable power of the Middle Kingdom.

"You have dissembled to us, disguising in your dispatches the true nature of affairs. Your official seals shall be immediately taken from you and with the speed of flames you shall hasten to Peking. Respect this!" read the Emperor's summons to Commissioner Lin.

It was only when British troops were on the Yangtze River, moving towards Nanking, that the Emperor acknowledged that the "displays of celestial terror" promised by Commissioner Lin (long since stripped of honours and banished to Turkestan) were not going to materialize. He dispatched commissioners to negotiate a settlement.

On 29th August 1842, Chinese and British officials gathered on board the flagship Cornwallis to sign the Treaty of Nanking. A twenty-one-gun salute officially marked the end of the Anglo-Chinese War.

The signing of the Treaty had implications for every foreign nation that had commercial or territorial

ambitions in the East. For although dubbed the "Opium War", the conflict had been as much about free trade as the illicit drug traded at Lintin. And although the initiator was Britain, every other nation represented in Canton would reap benefits from the Treaty's most significant clause: the opening of five treaty ports — Amoy, Foochow, Ningpo, Canton and Shanghai — to foreign trade.

From China's point of view, things would never be the same again. After centuries of knowing only the

The Treaty of Nanking, opened to foreign trade the ports of Amoy (above) and Foochow (left).

expansion of its power and influence, it was forced to tolerate foreigners, pursuing their passion for trade, in five of its principle ports. The Treaty had also forced it to relinquish, in perpetuity, one of its islands close to Canton.

Certainly the island itself was of little consequence: an insignificant corner of the empire, far removed from the capital, and a lair for troublesome pirates. Even the British Foreign Secretary, Lord Palmerston, was said to have scoffed at the "barren rock" of Hong Kong that would never become a mart of trade. And Queen Victoria was said to be much amused at the cession of this seemingly lustreless addition to her imperial crown.

Though the Emperor and Palmerston wrung their hands at the loss and acquisition of Hong Kong, others with vision saw its potential to become one of the glittering prizes of the British empire. The taipans had urged the need for an island based on the doorstep of China, and Hong Kong was blessed — as the luckless Lord Napier

had noted — with a "safe and commodious harbour". They presaged it would make a fine entrepôt port for British merchants, and for every nation that traded at Canton.

The Americans and French, Swedish and Russians were quick to negotiate their own separate treaties with China following the British victory. However, Britain enjoyed a "most favoured nation" status that entitled it to any concession granted to a rival.

And a clause negotiated by the Americans — guaranteeing toleration of missionaries — would light a beacon in the far-flung heathen empire that proved irresistible to Christians across the globe.

Saving the idol-worshipping Chinese became the passionate obsession of many. They crossed oceans, set up homes in often hostile towns, built churches, preached and prayed — and buried their children, in newly laid foreign cemeteries, far from home.

Their coming to China added yet another — spiritual — dimension to the encounter.

*Top: **Final salute to a fallen comrade at the naval cemetery at Weihaiwei.***
*Left: **Hong Kong's deep water harbour.***

THE ALIEN FAITHS

CHRISTIAN MISSIONARIES HAD BEEN ACTIVE IN CHINA FOR CENTURIES — INDEED THE earliest Christian monument dated back to the 8th century.

During the 17th and 18th centuries, Jesuits found considerable favour with the Court in Peking and, during this golden era, mandarin and missionary were enriched by a cultural exchange that seemed extraordinary to later evangelists. The Jesuits gave advice to the Emperor, were permitted to live in the capital, celebrated Mass publicly and preached, baptized and ministered to a Christian community of Chinese converts numbering three million.

Unlike those who succeeded them, the Jesuits appreciated that to become part of the fabric of Chinese society they had to shed elements of their faith. They also had to adopt a tolerant attitude towards other faiths. For the Chinese burnt joss sticks at the alters of innumerable gods, acknowledging that what separated Confucianism, Buddhism and Taoism was less important than what united them. "The three teachings flow into one," said their hosts, and the Jesuits saw this at funerals where rituals of Confucian filial piety were practised alongside those performed by Buddhist monks and Taoist priests.

So the Jesuits became tolerant and were tolerated. They dressed as mandarins, learnt the language, and read the classics that were the basis of learning for every Chinese scholar who rose to official power.

They also appreciated the potent appeal of colourful processions of bishops, the tolling of bells from fine cathedrals, and statues of the Virgin held high above the heads of children bearing candles.

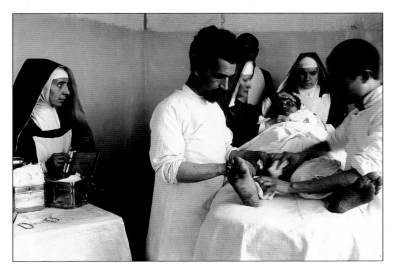

Perhaps it was success that doomed the Jesuits — in the eyes of purists and rivals — for the era of accord ended in unseemly squabbles. Tolerance was seen to compromise their faith and, when Rome intervened, they were recalled.

In Macao, a base for preparing priests for work in the interior, Jesuits were arrested and deported. The imposing St Paul's Church, its seminary acknowledged as the finest in Asia, was later destroyed by a spectacular fire in 1835. All

that remained was the ornate granite façade at the top of a grandiose sweep of steps. For some this would symbolize the slender achievements of the missionary movement in the years that followed.

The Jesuits left behind them communities of Catholics struggling to maintain an alien faith as the stream of missionaries from Europe dwindled and anti-foreign sentiment mounted. Faith was sustained by occasional clandestine visits of missionaries who washed their faces with tea, attached false queues beneath conical hats and donned Chinese gowns.

Sometimes the hard and lonely lives of these men ended in death and martyrdom. But when blood-stained robes were retrieved by the faithful and sent back to a distant homeland, they merely served to inspire others.

While the Catholics preferred to battle the unknown in the interior of China, the Protestants — prior to the opening of the treaty ports — were mainly based in Macao and Canton, along with the merchants.

The Protestants translated the Bible into Chinese characters — but, weighing five pounds, it was far less practical to distribute than religious tracts. The latter were produced in vast quantities by Protestant presses throughout Asia in the 19th century. However, there was little evidence that the printed word won converts — many a tract was destined to paper the walls and ceilings of humble Chinese homes.

Left: ***Italian medical missionaries.*** *Top:* ***The façade of Macao's St Paul's Church.***

"These Protestants simply will not see that Scripture by itself... can no more develop true faith and check error than a code of laws without judges," expostulated a Catholic missionary of the day.

More successful were the Protestant medical missionaries who lanced abscesses, excised tumours, restored sight and were generally appreciated by communities that came to depend on them.

George Morrison, the Australian correspondent for The Times of London, journeying through China in the latter half of the 19th century, would note: "The attitude of the Chinese is one of perfect friendliness towards the missionary, combined with perfect apathy towards his religion."

*W*hen the first five treaty ports opened following the Treaty of Nanking, the missionary presence in China received an enormous boost. Some of those who arrived at that time became well respected members of the community, others were involved in commendable charitable or medical works, but the majority laboured long for souls that proved elusive.

There were, however, occasional conversions that had spectacular — if unpredictable — repercussions.

When a Chinese Christian convert boldly distributed Christian tracts at the provincial examination hall in Canton before police pursued him, one fell into the hands of an ambitious candidate.

Hung Hsiu-ch'uan came from a village near Canton, the son of a Hakka peasant who spared no effort to provide the education that could lead to an official appointment. But, in the 1830s, Hung failed in the examination hall on many occasions. Racked with frustration, he experienced a profound spiritual revelation which prompted him to form a quasi-Christian movement. Eventually the movement became more military than spiritual, and so powerful it challenged the ruling dynasty.

Claiming direct communication with the Holy Trinity and implementing a strictly moral regime that outlawed opium smoking, foot binding and prostitution, Hung proclaimed himself the "Heavenly King". His militant message appealed not only to the impoverished Hakkas amongst whom he had lived, but to the disaffected of a society in ferment.

Defeat at the hands of the foreigners had cast doubt on the leadership of the Manchu elite and the strength of its once-proud Tatar army. Discontent was also underscored by the opening of the treaty ports to foreign trade. Whereas once all exports had moved through Canton, the shift to other ports put many Cantonese coolies and boatmen out of work. They were among the first to join Hung's rebels in the 1840s.

Support came also from other echelons of society. Scholars were outraged at the selling of civil offices to raise revenue; anti-Manchu secret society members were keen to capitalize on the rising nationalist sentiment; bandits were looking for action; and the numberless poor, their ranks swelled by the devastation of recent floods and droughts — all were drawn to the movement that promised land reform, a better way of life, and an end of Manchu rule and official corruption.

Selecting a name for his movement that conjured images of peace and plenty — Taiping — the failed scholar established a strictly disciplined rebel army that was soon on the move. Buoyed by the enthusiasm of its ever-growing recruits, it achieved astounding victories.

Foreign merchants and missionaries observed the Taiping rebel movement with mixed feelings. The anti-foreign stance of the Manchu rulers in Peking had not endeared the dynasty to foreigners. Merchants speculated that the Taiping ruler might be more amenable — and indeed the Governor of Hong Kong, Sir George Bonham, was the first foreign diplomat to make contact with the Taiping leadership after the rebels took Nanking in 1853.

Foreign missionaries speculated that the seed of Hung's idiosyncratic Christianity was at least widely sown in the alien land. With careful nurturing by foreign missionaries, it might be encouraged to flower in a more predictable way.

But there was nothing predictable about the Taiping movement. The optimism of onlookers soon turned to outrage as the now formidable rebel armies set about slaughtering — on a spectacular scale — any who opposed

*Top left: **The Times correspondent, Dr George Morrison, embarking on a journey through China.***
*Top: **Catholic street procession.***

them. By 1855 they controlled most of the fertile Lower Yangtze Valley.

Whereas once there had been a single leader, suddenly the Taiping leadership — like some monstrous Hydra — sprouted numerous heads: a king for every point of the compass, each with individual armies and ambitions.

The egalitarian principles that had been so appealing to supporters in the early days of the movement were rapidly jettisoned. Workers were soon labouring to build elaborate palaces in which Hung accommodated the concubines he publicly condemned. Though he seldom ventured beyond his palace walls, his subjects were in danger of immediate decapitation if they failed to abase themselves before his palanquin.

Eventually the areas surrounding the Taiping strongholds were gripped by fear, for it was reported that when the Taipings had captured Nanking the rebels had slaughtered the entire Tatar garrison plus their families — some twenty-five thousand people. And the devastated countryside was alive with rumours of plots and counterplots being hatched among the feuding Taiping leaders; and of bloody reprisals against any town that did not submit to the will of the Taiping leader.

Foreign observers, repelled by the reported carnage, quickly realized that the movement had degenerated into wild fanaticism. "They do nothing but burn, murder and destroy," noted a British diplomat in Peking. They also disrupted trade — which could not be tolerated. There was even talk of military intervention

to help the Emperor restore order.

But foreign attention was at that time focused elsewhere, for frustration was mounting at China's dilatory attitude towards implementing the Treaty of Nanking.

Fourteen years after it had been signed, foreign merchants were still unable to live in Canton, though the other treaty ports accommodated foreign residences and consulates. In 1848 the irascible Yeh Ming-ch'en was appointed Imperial Commissioner of Canton, and his intense dislike of foreigners was only exceeded by his ingenuity in dreaming up incidents which would restrict them to the factory area that was the source of so much frustration.

*H*aving dealt China its first defeat at the hands of a Western power in the Opium War, the merchants at Canton fully expected their status to be amended. Contempt, they hoped, would give way to civility, even respect.

However, Commissioner Yeh treated them with arrogant disdain; the gentry and people stubbornly resisted the entry of foreigners into the city; and posters threatening their extermination papered the city walls. One incident after another exacerbated the always abrasive relationship between merchant and mandarin.

When, in October 1856, the police boarded a Hong Kong-registered vessel, the Arrow, anchored opposite the factories, arresting several members of the crew, the incident became yet another convenient "insult to the flag". Once again British warships moved up the Pearl River to silence the cannons at the Lion's Gate forts.

Commissioner Yeh had offered a bounty for every English head brought to him and sent an angry throng to torch the factories. As flames consumed the symbol of the hated foreign presence on Chinese soil, claiming the lives of several English consular staff, they also unleashed anti-foreign sentiment in neighbouring Hong Kong. Attempts were made to poison several of the fledgling colony's top officials; assaults became commonplace; and when several Europeans were decapitated by Chinese sailors on a steamer, an appeal for help went out to the Governor of India and to Britain's Foreign Secretary, Lord Palmerston.

Merchants calling for strong action found an ally in the Governor of Hong Kong, Sir John Bowring, who pressed the view that China would not change its anti-foreign stance until foreign troops occupied the city of Canton.

When in 1857 the China Question was debated in the House of Commons, Palmerston's rhetoric had much the same affect as Macaulay's had in 1840. The Commissioner of Canton had violated the British flag, disregarded treaties, offered rewards for the heads of British subjects and planned their destruction by "murder, assassination and poison".

The British public had been alternately intrigued and outraged by events in China, ever since Commissioner Lin had destroyed the British opium. So famous had Lin become that he and his wife were featured in Madame Tussaud's as "The Author of the Chinese War and his Small Footed Wife".

*Top left: **Buddhist monks at Chengdu monastery.** Left: **Looters arrested during an uprising.***

In London, the man in the street shared Queen Victoria's view that those who considered Governor Bowring's stance as "menacing and arrogant" were unpatriotic bores. They rallied to the Foreign Secretary's conclusion that the time was ripe to "strike another blow at China".

And when the grisly details of the death of a French missionary began to fill newspapers in both Paris and London, further fuel was added to the call to arms.

Abbe Chapdeleine had been preaching in Kwangsi province — beyond the limits of the treaty ports opened to foreigners — when arrested, tortured and decapitated in February 1857. According to his superior, his heart was "torn out of his chest and, still beating, chopped into pieces, fried in a pan with pig's grease and was eaten."

The two nations that had achieved victory in the Crimean War were determined to mount an expeditionary force that would avenge the lives lost — and at the same time attempt to open further ports to trade.

Lord Elgin, Queen Victoria's plenipotentiary, hastened to Hong Kong, but lost most of his troops en route when they were diverted to deal with a mutiny in India. Baron Gros, France's Commissaire-extraordinaire, took his time and it was months before the allied men-of-war stormed Canton and took it with ease, in December 1857.

Commissioner Yeh was captured, put aboard HMS Inflexible and shipped to India, where he died in exile. With the troublesome Commissioner out of the way, order was restored so rapidly that the allied officers and troops were soon enjoying visits to Canton's tea gardens, local curio shops and markets.

The expeditionary force then moved north to the mouth of the Peiho River and Elgin dispatched a letter to Peking, written with the support of the French, Russian and American Ministers, to request negotiation for a new treaty. When this was rejected, the Taku forts were attacked and taken so easily that Lord Elgin speculated: "Twenty-four men with revolvers and a sufficient number of cartridges might walk through China from one end to the other."

When Elgin threatened to march on Peking, the Chinese authorities agreed to the terms of the Treaty of Tientsin, signed in June 1858. Similar treaties were also signed between China and France, America and Russia.

The Treaty of Tientsin achieved the allied aims. Ten more treaty ports ranging from Manchuria to Formosa were opened to trade, including four on the Yangtze River. The Treaty also gained other important rights for foreigners: disputes involving foreign subjects would be dealt with by their own officials (and, where Chinese subjects were involved, by a mixed court); Christianity was to be tolerated and protected; foreign travel in the interior of China was permitted; and a foreigner was never again to be described as a "barbarian" in official documents.

Agreement was also reached in regard to the residence of an ambassador in Peking, but Elgin allowed himself to be persuaded by Chinese officials that to immediately implement this

Francis Beato's classic photograph of carnage at the Taku forts.

further sign of the humbling of the empire would undermine the stability of the government.

Opium also featured in the Treaty with the legalization of the trade which had steadily increased despite the opening of the treaty ports. This controversial move acknowledged the difficulty of suppressing the trade and was defended on the grounds that at least it put the revenue from import duties into the hands of the Chinese government, rather than the pockets of corrupt officials.

A year after it was signed, representatives of Britain and France prepared to sail up the Peiho to ratify the Treaty of Tientsin. On arrival at the mouth of the river they found it blockaded and the Taku forts rebuilt and strengthened.

Assured that this action had been taken to ward off an attack by Taiping rebels, they were invited to proceed to Peking overland, leaving their gunboats behind. The American Minister agreed — and was subjected to the discomfort on an unsprung cart and an irritating debate about the ceremonial kowtow at the end of the journey. The allies refused.

Lord Elgin's brother, Frederick Bruce, who had been appointed British Envoy Extraordinary and British Minister in China, no doubt recalled stories of the first easy conquest of the Taku forts the previous year. So without

much ado he ordered Admiral Sir James Hope to clear the river blockade, so that he could proceed to Tientsin. Six hundred marines and a company of engineers were dispatched to remove the obstructions — until Chinese guns opened fire from the forts and their gunboats were forced to retreat.

The Admiral rashly pressed on with the attack, and landing troops came under heavy fire on the muddy foreshore. American military observers briefly abandoned their neutrality to help retrieve the wounded as the British counted the cost of the action. Four ships had been sunk, two were badly damaged, Hope was severely wounded and there were over four hundred casualties.

While The Times applauded Admiral Hope's audacity, other newspapers were not so laudatory, questioning the tactics that had "so gloriously buried the British forces in the mud."

Fresh troops were summoned to restore allied honour (eleven thousand British and Indian troops, seven thousand French), but the massive force approaching his shores in no way influenced the Chinese Emperor to accept an allied ultimatum.

As he approached Hong Kong in 1859 at the head of the new force, Lord Elgin chastised himself as the "greatest fool that the world ever saw" for having accepted this second mission to China. For the Scot had taken an instant dislike to the Governor, Sir John Bowring, and the foreign merchants based in Hong Kong. He had found his countrymen "overbearing, arrogant and vindictive", and Bowring's constant tirades so tiresome that during his earlier visit he had abandoned plans to stay at Government House. Instead he endured the cramped accommodation afforded by his frigate in the stifling heat of mid-summer.

For their part the merchants and officials of Hong Kong found Elgin's approach too mild and conciliatory. His opponents made much of the fact that he had given in to the Chinese on the question of stationing an ambassador in Peking.

When the Anglo-French expeditionary force arrived at the Taku forts, the mud flats that had claimed so many lives during the previous humiliating assault once again plagued them. Soldiers struggled with sinking gun carriages and cavalry horses floundered knee-deep in the mire.

However, the first engagement with imperial troops at Taku gave them a decisive victory and their commanders noted with pride that the Chinese cavalry mounted on small Mongolian ponies were no match for the Sikhs and Dragoons on heavy chargers. But taking the forts was no easy task for they were as difficult to assault as they were to abandon.

The Emperor's troops fought bravely and more than a thousand died — some lashed by their officers to cannon so that they could not flee the allied bombardment or the bayonets that followed as the forts were stormed.

*Top: **Lord Elgin's headquarters**. Right: **Foreign troops outside Peking's Forbidden City**.*

When the heavy smoke lifted from the crenellated walls of the forts, the carnage provided a gruesome collection of images for the Italian photographer Francis Beato who came to China as the semi-official photographer of the Anglo-French expeditionary force.

Several awards for gallantry celebrated the bravery of the invaders who had stormed the forts and taken them at a cost of thirty-four lives, evenly divided between the allies.

*L*ess evenly divided was the plunder that the two armies extracted from the towns they subsequently occupied as the forces moved towards the Chinese capital. Each army accused the other of avarice and looting, and the streets of occupied towns occasionally became the backdrop for bizarre parades as French troopers minced in silks and fans through streets littered with plunder.

British commanders had looters severely flogged, but no such discipline was exercised over French troops. Observing their actions, a British soldier expressed a fervent wish, shared by colleagues, "that our own favoured land may ever be spared from such scenes of desolation."

As the allies approached Peking, they were assured by high-ranking mandarins sent to negotiate that the requisite treaties would be ratified and all their demands met. However, within the purple-stained walls of the Forbidden City a war of words raged between princes and scholars, courtiers and concubines.

There were those who advocated tolerance of the foreigners, arguing that, unlike other invaders, they demanded nothing more than the right to trade free. Some officials even urged the Emperor to apply the skills of the Western world to strengthen his own empire.

But other, shriller voices denied that the Middle Kingdom had anything to learn from the invaders. The hawks within the Court had taken heart at the first defeat that imperial troops had handed to the allies at

the Taku forts the previous summer. They urged a spirited defence, seeing in such action a chance to revive the military glory of the early years of Manchu rule.

But the Ch'ing army was no longer the force it once had been. Revenues had been dissipated on imperial pleasures, the army was ill-equipped and the descendants of the Manchu soldiers and generals were not the battle-hardened, dedicated warriors that had seized the Dragon Throne centuries earlier.

But the empire still boasted military leaders of courage and brilliance, such as the Mongolian commander Seng-ko-lin-ch'in. It was Seng who had rebuilt and strengthened the Taku forts and then been forced to abandon them. Now he urged the Emperor to resist the invaders and eventually his counsel prevailed at Court.

While this change of heart took place within the walls of the Forbidden City, a party of allied officers were still involved in negotiating peace. Lord Elgin's Private Secretary, Harry Loch, and other negotiators were still wrangling with Chinese counterparts over Treaty terms and arrangements for Elgin's arrival in Peking, when Seng's troops began massing outside the capital.

The Chinese commander was confident. He knew the allied forces were small compared with the thousands he could muster. He also knew that their leaders, so confident in Chinese assurances of peace, had left heavy artillery and large supplies of ammunition behind them as they approached Peking.

Meanwhile British and French troops, appreciating that the situation had changed dramatically, had launched their attack against an estimated twenty-thousand Chinese troops, outnumbered five to one.

Both sides fought fiercely — the imperial troops because they were defending the seat of the Dragon Throne, heart of their once-proud empire; the allies because they were outraged at the perceived duplicity of their enemy — and at the unknown fate of the party of negotiators who, carrying a flag of truce, had been captured by the enemy.

As in other battles the poorly-manned Chinese cannons fired shells that invariably flew over the heads of the advancing troops. "It was like fighting in a dream: we kept advancing, firing and killing the enemy, yet no one, or hardly anyone, was hurt in our own ranks," recalled a French observer. Once again a thousand Chinese dead littered the battlefield, while allied losses were minimal.

After a particularly brutal battle on a bridge just outside the capital, valiantly defended by Chinese troops, the injured commander ordered the execution of some of the foreign prisoners. A French priest and a captain of the Royal Artillery were both beheaded on the bridge. It was an action that would have historic repercussions.

With the victorious allies only a few miles from the capital, the Emperor Hsien-feng wanted only to abandon his capital and retreat beyond the Great Wall to his northern palace at Jehol. There he could forget the threat of the allies, and the shrill advice of his favourite concubine. At Jehol there were rugged hills and forests, boar and deer to be hunted, and the pavilions and lakes that pleased his pleasure-loving court.

When he knew the allies had triumphed, and could now march on to the capital, his entourage departed in disarray. He left his capital — and the settlement of peace — in the hands of his younger half-brother, Prince Kung.

Negotiations now sped between Prince Kung and Lord Elgin, as the allied troops planned to rendezvous at Peking's fabled Summer Palace of Yuan-ming Yuan. The British troops arrived a day after the French to discover that the treasures held within this undefended complex had proved irresistible to them.

A bemused French count reported the "strange and unforgettable vision" of his nation's troops pillaging the palace. "Some soldiers had buried their heads in the red-lacquered chests of the Empress," remembered Count d'Herisson. "Others were half-hidden among heaps of embroidered fabrics and silkware, still others were filling their pockets, shirts and kepis with rubies, sapphires, pearls and pieces of crystal."

The surfeit of wealth turned them into "grown children" he said, and their laughter and shouts of glee mingled with the chiming of hundreds of ornamental clocks, the repetitive refrains of thousands of musical boxes, and the sounds of smashing porcelain. There was such an abundance of gold that the French concluded it was fake, and cast it away, concentrating instead on smashing clocks to retrieve their jewels, gathering armfuls of silk, jade, cloisonné and other riches as they moved from room to room in their feverish search for treasure.

When the astonished British arrived on the scene, they encountered a spectacle of such devastation that few would forget that first impression of what had once been the Emperor of China's favourite retreat.

But Lord Elgin would later write: "There was not a room that I saw in which half the things had not been taken away or broken to pieces... Plundering and devastating a place like this is bad enough, but what is much worse is the waste and breakage... French soldiers were destroying in every way the most beautiful silks, breaking the jade ornaments and porcelain. War is a hateful business... The more one sees of it, the more one detests it."

The fabled Summer Palace in the hills beyond Peking.

The Burning of The Summer Palace

THE DAY AFTER THE SUMMER PALACE HAD BEEN SACKED, THE SURVIVORS OF THE NEGOTIATING PARTY — seized by Chinese troops prior to the battle on the outskirts of the capital — were released on the orders of Prince Kung.

When the British consular official Harry Parkes, Lord Elgin's private secretary Henry Loch, and a small party of troops saw the gates of the Forbidden City open and close to allow them to rejoin their forces, they felt intense relief that their ordeal was over. But they left behind a party of British, French and Sikhs who had not survived their capture. The chilling tale the party told on arrival would further seal the fate of the Summer Palace.

When the Chinese arrested the group — carrying a flag of truce and trying to return to the allied camp — they assumed that Parkes held an exalted position, for his fluency in Chinese assured him a key position in negotiations. They even suspected that he controlled the movement of the allied troops. Parkes was therefore singled out for interrogation and ill-treatment, but as Loch recorded, "maintained outwardly an appearance of calm indifference to all that could be done to him."

Parkes, who later became Sir Harry Parkes, Shanghai Consul, was a skilful linguist in the consular service, but like many a foreigner he knew little of the elaborate web of etiquette that prescribed so much of Chinese behaviour. Having for many years watched foreign diplomats wallow in what seemed like the nightmare evasiveness of Chinese diplomacy, Parkes believed that surrendering any ground at the negotiating table was perceived as weakness. His uncompromising code of conduct earned him the dislike of Chinese officials — and no doubt dictated the cool arrogance that carried him through interrogation and imprisonment, when iron fetters secured him to the ceiling of his cell.

Less fortunate than Parkes and Loch were those, including The Times correspondent, who never lived to recount the horrors of their ordeal. Tales of cords bound so tightly they cut into flesh, inviting the feasting of maggots and a slow death; of decapitation and death by the sword; of burial up to the neck in dirt, to be savaged by dogs, soon aroused indignation through the allied camps.

Having reached an accord with Prince Kung on most of the provisions of the peace agreement, there was no question of mounting an allied attack on Peking. But the treachery of the prisoners' treatment demanded some form of retribution.

The leader of the British forces knew that demands for an indemnity would cost the Emperor nothing, for the burden of raising the money would inevitably fall on the people. He suspected that calls for the mandarins responsible would merely result in him being handed scapegoats. He concluded that destroying the Summer Palace would be "the least objectionable of several courses."

As the palatial palace had witnessed the torture of several of the prisoners who had later died, its destruction was appropriate. "The punishment," he concluded, "was one which would fall not on the people, but exclusively on the Emperor" in robbing him of a favourite playground.

The Summer Palace first began to take shape in the hills five miles from Peking during the 18th century. Successive rulers had embellished the summer retreat, adding pavilions and temples, gardens of flowering shrubs and rare trees. They filled the artificial lakes with glimmering goldfish; ornamental ducks nested in the reeds; and antlered deer roamed on the banks.

When members of Lord Macartney's mission to China had first seen the Summer Palace, they had marvelled at its gilded halls, marble floors and the fabulous spread of Argus pheasant tail fans that framed the Emperor's throne. It had seemed a perfect symbol of the wealth and beauty of the Middle Kingdom.

Now, sixty years later, a young officer of the Royal Engineers was moving his men resolutely through the complex, putting torches to the drapes and polished timber. "You can scarcely imagine the beauty and magnificence

The palace in the hills outside Peking — the summer retreat of the Imperial household.

of the palaces we burnt," recorded an officer of the Royal Engineers. "It made one's heart sore."

For two days the flames raged and the pillars of dense smoke spiralled. Those who watched from Peking felt the bitter rain of cinders as smoke darkened the sky above the capital. And within days of its destruction, there was more humiliation. The streets of the capital echoed to the sound of advancing regimental bands, cavalry and infantry as Lord Elgin's palanquin approached Peking's Hall of Ceremonies.

It was a moment of unqualified triumph for the allies, so long discounted as uncivilized "barbarians"; a time of bitter defeat for the government of China.

The Convention of Peking, signed in late October 1860, confirmed and extended the provisions of the Tientsin Treaty. Tientsin was opened to foreign trade, and the precocious entrepôt port of Hong Kong was expanded to embrace the Kowloon peninsula that had been leased temporarily as a military camp for the expeditionary forces. Missionaries were permitted to buy land and build churches throughout the empire; foreign powers were allowed to base representatives in the Chinese capital; and there was the bonus of an indemnity of several million dollars for each of the victorious allies — to add to the plunder from the Summer Palace.

While Prince Kung and Lord Elgin indulged in strained ceremonials in Peking, the Emperor Hsien-feng and his retinue languished at the northern palace at Jehol. Among his party was a concubine who had enjoyed great favour with the Emperor — but whose standing, within his coterie, had been soured by her spirited appeals

against his shameful flight from the capital.

For a concubine of the second rank, Tz'u-hsi, the daughter of a minor Manchu official, had achieved remarkable influence in Court circles. Her chief assets were the heir she had produced for the Emperor; a temper that made her widely feared at Court; and a single-minded ruthlessness that would see her dispatch, with ingenuity and efficiency, any who attempted to thwart her ambition. Such qualities guaranteed her a prominent role in the dying decades of the Ch'ing dynasty.

When within a year of the signing of the Convention of Peking the pleasure-loving Emperor lay dead, a victim of his profligate lifestyle, rival princes plotted the demise of the precocious concubine. But with the help of a dashing Manchu army captain, Jung-lu, whispered to be her childhood sweetheart, Tz'u-hsi survived. While the plotters were committing suicide or being decapitated, she assumed the title of Empress Dowager and regent for her five-year-old son.

Certainly she was supposed to share power with her cousin, who had enjoyed higher rank as Empress Consort, but the placid nature of the latter ensured that her voice would seldom be heard.

From the outset of her regency the Empress Dowager Tz'u-hsi determined that no force would rob her of her newly acquired authority —particularly not the Taiping rebels whose disruption of the empire had spanned a decade. Hung, the Taiping leader, continued to promote himself as a heaven-sent prophet, and a future Emperor of China, from his capital at Nanking. And his rebels continued to devastate one of the nation's most fertile regions, the Yangtze Valley.

The Empress Dowager was determined to crush the Taipings — and in this she found common ground with the foreigners she so detested. In battling the Taiping forces, imperial and foreign troops would work together for the first time to rid the empire of an enemy that threatened its stability — and the potential prosperity of the newly opened treaty ports.

*W*eeks before the allies torched the Summer Palace, the Taiping rebels had attacked Shanghai. When the young Major Charles George Gordon arrived in the treaty port in September 1860, he noted the grisly sight of rebel heads displayed in baskets on the city walls. "The rebels are reported to be about fifteen miles from this settlement," noted Gordon as he prepared to travel north to join Lord Elgin's force.

During the Taiping attack on Shanghai, the most prosperous treaty port, a combined Anglo-Chinese force had repelled the attack. But residents of the city could not relax, for stories of the fanatical, long-haired rebels flooded the city with each wave of newly arrived refugees. And the town of Soochow, centre of the prosperous silk industry — not more than fifty miles away — was in rebel hands.

The International Settlement in Shanghai could call upon a small garrison of British and French troops, a small naval squadron and a corps of volunteers when threatened by Taiping rebels. But the battle-hardened rebels were increasingly well-armed — and were supplied with modern weapons by unscrupulous foreign merchants in

Indian expeditionary forces enter Peking.

both Shanghai and Hong Kong.

To bolster the defence of the treaty port, foreign merchants put up the money for a force of mercenaries that called itself the Ever Victorious Army — "a name to be taken not in a literal but in a transcendental and Celestial sense," noted a local newspaper. The exploits of this fighting force — its officers composed of a cosmopolitan band of soldiers of fortune, its ranks of Chinese soldiers attracted by generous rates of pay — had soon attracted the attention of an ambitious young Chinese commander, Li Hung-chang, who would rise to become one of the most powerful figures in the Empress Dowager's inner circle during her five decades of power.

Li Hung-chang was also a skilful negotiator who communicated well with the foreign powers he dealt

with. When he went to Shanghai to request that the Ever Victorious Army fight alongside Imperial forces he received a sympathetic hearing. The Chinese commander offered to pay the mercenary force, a ploy which he exploited when he wanted to direct its course of action. He also requested that it be led by a British officer from the Royal Engineers — but when Major Charles

George Gordon assumed command, Li encountered an idealist who would prove impossible to manipulate.

"It is a direct blessing from Heaven, the coming of this British Gordon. He is superior in manner and bearing to any foreigner I have come in contact with, and does not show outwardly that conceit which makes most of them repugnant in my sight..." declared Li Hung-chang.

Deeply religious and extremely demanding of himself and his men, Gordon moulded his unruly soldiers into a formidable fighting force. The young commander appreciated — as had his hero, Giuseppe Garibaldi — that the leader of irregular troops had to master a multitude of skills from planning and preparing his attack to leading his men into battle. And when he did the latter Gordon was always conspicuously to the fore, brandishing nothing more lethal than his cane. His courage seemed boundless, his life charmed and he gave great heart to his troops.

Shortly before he encountered Major Gordon for the first time, Li Hung-chang fulminated in his diary against the superior airs of foreigners. However, the thirty-year-old British major prompted a quite different response. "Within two hours after his arrival he was inspecting the troops and giving orders; and I could not but rejoice at the manner in which his commands were obeyed," recorded Li.

Gordon employed considerable strategy when planning his attacks on the heavily defended walled cities that were rebel strongholds. He drew up battle plans after surveying the site himself and often moved and deployed his troops under cover of darkness.

Sometimes so decisive was the initial assault that victory was swift and loss of life minimal. Occasionally rebel towns surrendered before the battle had begun, having heard that the leader of the Ever Victorious Army was humane and refused to sanction the massacre of prisoners. Indeed, when a massacre was carried out by Li's Imperial troops, the outraged Gordon threatened to abandon his force. But the battle against the rebels was at a crucial point, and Gordon remained at his post.

By now the Imperial forces and the Ever Victorious Army had forced the rebels back towards their capital, Nanking, where the final battles were fought in July 1864. Hung, the Taiping's "Heavenly King", poisoned himself

with gold leaf and several of his wives hung themselves over his grave. It was a grisly end to a violent era that, in its final days alone, cost an estimated one hundred thousand lives.

The Empress Dowager made much of her role in the defeat of the rebels, but the legacy of the Taipings would haunt her declining dynasty. For the provincial armies under Chinese commanders could as easily be turned against the house of Ch'ing in the future.

With the enemy vanquished — the Ever Victorious Army being disbanded even before the fall of Nanking —

Gordon was honoured with the highest rank in the Chinese army. He refused all other rewards, and unlike many who served his government in the East, returned home a poorer man than when he had left.

For a while he worked in obscurity, helping the poor and working for the church. Later he served in the Sudan — and the man who had eluded the Russians at Sebastopol and the Taipings in China, fell to the spear of an African dervish, on the steps of his remote palace. The man known to the troops of the Ever Victorious Army as Chinese Gordon, became known to the world as Gordon of Khartoum.

*Left: **Guards of the American opium trading firm, Russell and Company.***
*Above: **Major Charles George "Chinese" Gordon and his bodyguards.***

THE T'UNG-CHIH RESTORATION

WHEN THE BITTER MEMORY OF THE DESTRUCTION OF THE SUMMER PALACE BEGAN TO FADE, AND THE SCARS of the long Taiping rebellion began to heal, the Ch'ing dynasty enjoyed the balm of a renaissance that briefly slowed its inevitable decline.

At first the two Empress Dowagers were receptive to the advice of their chief counsellor, Prince Kung, during daily audiences at dawn when they sat behind a gold curtain symbolizing their regency.

Prince Kung had made considerable efforts to acquaint himself with the workings of foreign tariffs and trade — subjects that the literati still considered too base to warrant interest. The late Emperor's younger half-brother was fascinated by the advances made by Western nations and came to value the advice of foreign officials, such as the young Irishman Robert Hart who had joined the British consular service.

Hart was a rarity in that era of encounter — a foreigner fluent in Chinese and with a great love of China. But he was also a product of the Industrial Revolution and as such was committed to the new gods of science and technology. He earnestly wished China to share their gifts of Progress and Prosperity, and in this found common ground with the Manchu prince who invited him to become a servant of the Chinese empire.

At twenty-six Hart was appointed Inspector General of Chinese Customs and his efficient management of the revenue collection from foreign trade proved to be a financial mainstay for the dynasty. Eventually he spent over fifty years in China, serving first the British, then the Chinese government. As Sir Robert Hart, he was the doyen of the foreign community in Peking, noted for his great knowledge of the empire, his loyalty to the Empress Dowager, his sartorial elegance and his energetic promotion of the Chinese brass bands he established.

The rapport that developed between Hart and Prince Kung — the enthusiastic Irishman and the enlightened Manchu prince, both in their twenties, and both intrigued by their cultural differences — reflected a wider attitude of reconciliation that flowered during the 1860s and '70s.

The foreign powers in general welcomed the

emergence of Prince Kung, who was willing to have dialogue with the growing number of foreign diplomats in Peking — and both Britain and America championed a policy of cooperation with Chinese officials and support for the Ch'ing Court.

Under the influence of Prince Kung and the powerful Viceroy Li Hung-chang, students were encouraged to study abroad; a Chinese mandarin was dispatched to Europe as the empire's first unofficial envoy, and a Bureau of Foreign Affairs was established.

With the Empress Dowagers content to accept advice from the Grand Council and Prince Kung, and the foreign powers content to abide by the rules of the treaties, a sense of renewal imbued the house of Ch'ing. The title of the young Emperor's reign, T'ung-chih — "Return to Order" — promoted this sense of restoration.

The T'ung-chih Restoration was also infused with the awakening of interest in the West among a growing number of young scholars such as Soochow's Feng Kuei-fen. Feng coined the phrase "self-strengthening" and called

Left: **The Emperor's younger half-brother, Prince Kung.** *Top:* **Chinese customs office at Amoy.**
Above: **Sir Robert Hart, Inspector General of Chinese Customs.**

on his fellow men to study the sciences, to build shipyards and arsenals, and to expand educational horizons beyond the classical texts and calligraphy.

Li Hung-chang, who was appointed Viceroy of Chihli as a reward for his role in crushing the Taiping rebellion, used his provincial power and his influence at Court to steer the empire down the road of modernization. He quickly became China's chief negotiator with foreign powers and evinced an entrepreneurial flair that made him see the potential for profit — for himself and China — in a whole range of enterprises, from mines to merchant fleet, from trains to telegraphs.

As "self-strengthening" gathered force, arsenals and shipyards were built, and fortifications were strengthened. The French advised on building an arsenal at Foochow which became the pride of the T'ung-chih Restoration. Port Arthur and Weihaiwei, sited on the strategically important Bay of Pechili that gave access to

*Above: **The first Chinese embassy to visit the United States in 1868.***
*Left: **Shanghainese students departing for the United States — and a foreign education.***

Peking, were strengthened, as was Taku. Orders for steamships and gunboats were placed for the Chinese Navy.

Those who espoused the gospels of reform and Westernization believed that if the empire was to survive it needed to follow the example of Russia's Peter the Great and Japan's reformist Emperor Meiji. In the years to come both these nations would exploit the weakness of China, extracting territorial and other concessions — as had the European powers now firmly entrenched in the treaty ports.

The treaty ports themselves quickly became principal points of encounter between China and the foreign powers. They offered a window on the West — on republics and constitutional monarchies and democracies that were the chosen system of governments in these nations. And because the treaty ports also enjoyed extraterritoriality — the right of foreign residents to be tried under their own laws and to be immune from Chinese jurisdiction — they offered freedoms not available in Manchu China.

But this era of entente and intellectual encounter were bound to be overtaken by the more dramatic encounters that were inevitable in an age of imperialism — and in an empire where four hundred million Chinese were growing restless under a Manchu elite of five million.

And while there might have been common ground between a Manchu prince, a young Chinese reformer, an Irish customs chief and a powerful provincial Chinese viceroy — all would work within the shadow of the woman who dominated the last decades of the dynasty.

Top: **Members of the Chinese Customs at Tsingtao.** *Top right:* **Pupils of Queen's College in Hong Kong.**
Right: **Foreign employees of the Chinese Customs in Peking, with their Chinese teacher.**

THE EMPRESS DOWAGER

WHEN THE AMBITIOUS TZ'U-HSI AND THE GENTLE NIUHURU ASSUMED THE AUTHORITY OF co-regents to the Dragon Throne in 1861, they found themselves at the helm of an empire weakened by the protracted tyranny of the Taiping rebellion.

Large tracts of unproductive land encircled cities and villages that had been devastated by the Taiping rebels. During the years of the rebellion some six hundred walled cities were occupied — first captured by rebels, then claimed by Imperial troops. Some changed hands as many as three times — and each convulsion shattered families, scattered populations and left rice bowls empty.

Peking's Forbidden City was well and truly isolated from this world of suffering. Its walls encompassed a picture-book expanse of palaces and landscaped gardens built in the 15th century with a conscripted workforce of ten thousand craftsmen and a million labourers. Once created, no commoner set foot within its hallowed walls — all they

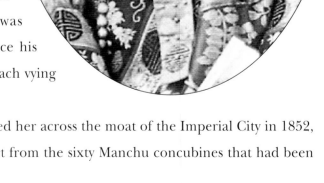

could glimpse of the Son of Heaven's earthly abode was the mellow gold of its roof tiles.

Though craftsmen had ornamented the palaces with celestial symbols, the Forbidden City was in reality a hothouse of gossip, graft and power play. The imperial household was dominated by three thousand eunuchs, each trying to advance his fortune; and a coterie of high pedigree Manchu concubines, each vying for the attention of the only able-bodied male: the Emperor.

From the day the imperial yellow sedan chair had carried her across the moat of the Imperial City in 1852, sixteen-year-old Tz'u-hsi had evinced qualities that set her apart from the sixty Manchu concubines that had been selected for the Emperor.

*Above: **The Empress Dowager.** Top right: **Eunuch Shao Xinglu.** Right: **The Forbidden City.***

Like them she was encased in silks, her skin was powdered white, her lips painted, her hair dressed with jade pins or fresh flowers. But while they gossiped and embroidered, she explored the vast libraries of the Forbidden City and cultivated powerful eunuchs who would later be her allies and spies. In a household of some three thousand women, she knew she would have to shape her own destiny — for some concubines never met the Emperor, let alone shared his bed.

Gossip had always surrounded the precocious concubine and it was rumoured that her personal eunuchs had lured the Emperor to a garden courtyard where he found her singing. She was summoned in the time-honoured way: her name was written on a jade tablet — for the eunuchs kept dates and details of all who shared the Dragon Bed — and the Chief Eunuch wrapped her in a scarlet rug and carried her to the Emperor's chamber.

Perhaps, along with the classics, the quick-witted concubine had also studied the numerous Taoist handbooks that described in lingering detail, the most adventurous and satisfying variations of love-making: "The Dragon Turns", "The White Tiger Leaps" and "The Butterfly Somersaults".

Certainly Tz'u-hsi pleased the Son of Heaven whose sexual appetite was already jaded by the harlots and transvestites of the Chinese city that lay beyond the walls of the Forbidden City. Their union resulted in Tz'u-hsi's promotion — to a concubine of the second rank — and her pregnancy.

Nine months later she presented the Emperor with a son — something his consort, the gentle Empress Niuhuru, had failed to achieve.

Her status within the Emperor's inner circle now assured, Tz'u-hsi was drawn irresistibly into the political orbit. But while her lively curiosity amused the Emperor, it aroused the antagonism of ministers, inured to treating women with Confucian contempt.

When the Emperor died, Tz'u-hsi had her first intoxicating taste of real power — and the pleasure of seeing her generals defeat the Taipings in 1864. But rebellions and discontent continued to debilitate the empire and the Empress Dowager — along with the Manchu elite who ruled China — continued to ignore the warning signals. Their only response was to dispatch the imperial army to crush each new rebellion.

When the T'ung-chih Emperor was ready to assume the throne in 1873 at the age of seventeen, Tz'u-hsi was reluctant to relinquish the power she had come to enjoy. However, her son's debauchery sapped him of much of his strength and in less than two years he lay dead. It was whispered in the teahouses that a towel tainted by smallpox had induced the "visitation of celestial flowers" that caused his death, and that it had been administered by his own mother — but then Tz'u-hsi had always generated gossip.

With the subsequent suicide of his consort, the Empress Dowagers graciously consented to a second regency — reiterating the assurance given in 1861 that as soon as a new Emperor was able to assume the reins of power, they would withdraw. In fact Niuhuru would soon succumb to a mysterious ailment which left Tz'u-hsi as the sole regent and supreme ruler of China.

In selecting an heir to the Dragon Throne, Tz'u-hsi felt sufficiently secure to break with tradition, choosing her own nephew over others with stronger claims. Her action outraged the mandarins and generated fierce debate, but the council responsible for nominating the successor knew better than to cross the Empress Dowager.

Enveloped in silks and fur, the bewildered three-year-old was brought to court in the imperial yellow sedan chair and the reign of the Kuang-hsu (Glorious Succession) Emperor began.

During her second regency, not even the occasional brave rebukes of counsellors or the court's lavish expenditure — estimated at over six million pounds annually — and its rumoured profligacy could undermine the Empress Dowager's authority.

Increasingly she surrounded herself with sycophants who neither challenged her decision-making, nor revealed to her the full extent of the calamities that ravaged the empire. Increasingly she indulged in the pleasures of her Court, promenading through the palace gardens with her retinue, swathed in silks and surmounted by parasols. Her favourite Chief

Eunuch was never far from her side (generating ribald speculation in the teahouses on whether he had undergone the brutal ritual that qualified castrati to live among the Emperor's concubines). And her handsome Manchu soldier, Jung-lu, was a trusted adviser and now a powerful military commander.

When Emperor Kuang-hsu was nineteen, Tz'u-hsi had already extended her regency as long as protocol would allow, and her nephew officially assumed the authority of the Dragon Throne. Although she moved her apartments in the Forbidden City to the Palace of Kindly and Tranquil Old Age, Tz'u-hsi continued her vice-like grip on power, perusing all government papers and making high-ranking appointments.

Surrounded by palace eunuchs who reported his every move to Tz'u-hsi, the Emperor cut a lonely figure. His only allies were the Pearl Concubine — who had the learning that Tz'u-hsi had craved as a young woman — and his tutor, Weng T'ung-ho. Along with the reformers who were gathering in the city beyond, the three had a fascination for Western ideas and technology. For in the last two decades of the century, the spring tide of reformist ideas was beginning to seriously challenge the traditions that had shaped China for so long.

In 1888, the young Emperor announced that the Summer Palace in the hills — destroyed by the allies in 1860 — was being restored and prepared as a garden palace for the Empress Dowager "for the cultivation of harmonious old age".

The Emperor's father, Prince Ch'un, had long been trying to lure the Empress Dowager from the seat of power so that his son might enjoy a measure of authority. But his success would cost the empire dearly.

For both the prince and Tz'u-hsi's loyal supporter Li Hung-chang had allowed her to siphon off Admiralty Board funds earmarked for her Empire's "self-strengthening". In particular, the funds had been intended to counter the rising naval power of the "dwarf barbarians" who were once again marshalling forces. This time their ambition centred on the citadel of Port Arthur.

*Left: **Tz'u-hsi's Marble Boat, built with money siphoned from naval funds.***
*Above: **Advisers to the Empress Dowager.***

THE RISING SUN

TZ'U-HSI'S SECOND REGENCY HAD BEGUN IN 1875, AND WITHIN A DECADE THE SUCCESSION of envoys that had once paid tribute to the Dragon Throne had declined. The Age of Empire was at its height, and the grab for power by Britain, France, Germany, Russia and Japan — that would mark the century's final decade — had begun in earnest.

It had been easy to plunder the outer limits of the vast empire of the Middle Kingdom. Weakened by war and rebellion, the crippling indemnities it paid to foreign powers, and by the corruption of a bureaucracy that reportedly pocketed as much as thirty per cent of revenue, China could do little to prevent its former satellites from moving beyond its orbit. Japan took the Ryukyu Islands, the British moved into Burma, the French into Annam (Vietnam) — and when China evinced a reluctance to accept the latter, the reduction to rubble of its proud new arsenal at Foochow (built with French advice) forced its hand.

The French grab for power in Annam sent the Empress Dowager into a fearful rage that saw her dismiss the entire Grand Council, plus Prince Kung. "Prince Kung at the outset of his career was wont to render us most zealous assistance, but this attitude became modified as time went by... to one of callous contentment with the sweets of

office..." she charged the prince.

Prince Kung had served the Dragon Throne for more than two decades and had been one of the few men not awed by the Empress Dowager. She replaced him and his fellow councillors with subjects who were — and began planning a lavish sixtieth birthday party for 1894. Officials were expected to donate one-quarter of their salaries to the Birthday Fund, but most — as was their custom — merely "squeezed" those below them for the requisite funds.

Processions of gift bearers began to make their way towards the Forbidden City through streets where the dusty bundles of abandoned babies were commonplace and parents sold their children rather than watch them

die. Silks and furs, jewels and delicacies were borne past mud-walled villages where there was never enough to eat and the chill of the advancing winter would claim the lives of the very young and old.

But as the winter of 1894 deepened, Tz'u-hsi's empire found itself once again at war — this time with its increasingly ambitious neighbour, Japan. The latter was well aware that China had long referred to it contemptuously as a nation of "dwarf barbarians" who had borrowed much of their language and culture from China.

Japan had made good use of Western technology and was now flexing its new-found military might and satisfying its own imperial ambitions. Already it had claimed sovereignty over the Ryukyu Islands that had paid tribute to China since the 14th century. Now the Land of the Rising Sun had ambitions to secure China's most strategic vassal, Korea. Patriotic Korean rebels were fighting to free their kingdom from

Left: *The Japanese Ambassador and his party visit south China.*
Above: *Formal opening of a Japanese-owned steel mill near Mukden, Manchuria.*

both its aspiring northern overlord and the empire to which it had traditionally kowtowed.

The conflict that ensued proved to be another humiliation for China. Despite the vaunted strength of the new northern army and navy that had so absorbed the energy of Viceroy Li Hung-chang, China was unable to hold either Port Arthur or the fortress of Weihaiwei, on the Kiaochow peninsula. Both guarded the gateway to the capital. Both had also been built with Western advice.

The Empress Dowager, ensconced in her Summer Palace restored with appropriated naval funds, reluctantly conceded to the cancellation of her lavish birthday celebrations. She expressed strong regret that the planned triumphal arches that were to have decorated the entire length of the Imperial Highway, from the capital to the Summer Palace, would not now be erected in her honour.

"Who would have anticipated that the dwarf men would have dared to force us into hostilities, and that since the beginning of summer they have invaded our tributary states and destroyed our fleet?" she lamented.

In the spring of 1895 the Treaty of Shimonoseki was signed, with Li Hung-chang conceding to Japanese demands for Formosa and the Pescadores off its west coast, and the opening of several treaty ports to Japan. With Formosa in the south and Korea in the north, Japan now had a solid base for future expansion — into Manchuria and China. It had also effectively replaced China as the major power in East Asia. Eager to thoroughly humiliate its once-haughty neighbour, Japan also demanded the secession of the Liaotung Peninsula on which Port Arthur was situated.

Although he agreed, Li Hung-chang trusted his instincts that the Western nations would not want the new imperial player to dominate such a strategic peninsula and to so radically alter the balance of power. He was right. Russia and Germany (both carving out "spheres of influence" in Manchuria and Shantung respectively) joined forces with France to persuade Japan to accept an additional war indemnity rather than the peninsula.

In the 20th century, Japan far outstripped its imperial rivals in establishing an industrial and commercial presence in the major cities of China and Taiwan.

Russia, in particular, was delighted when Japan agreed — for it had its own agenda for the peninsula. When the Empress Dowager dispatched Li Hung-chang to Russia for the coronation of Tsar Nicholas, Li — now widely accused of both graft and nepotism by his countrymen — negotiated an agreement that further enlarged his personal fortune and Russia's grand designs. Under the agreement, Russia obtained the right to extend the Trans-Manchurian Railway across two Chinese provinces. Soon Russia itself would lease the strategic peninsula and build a railway connection to Port Arthur.

Such high-handed actions always spurred the rival powers to extend their own territorial "spheres of influence"; demand further railway or mining concessions; or look for a suitable source of "provocation" which could generate military threats and further concessions.

The German Chancellor requested that his Minister in Peking "keep his eyes open for a suitable event as a cause for advance." Their objective was to demand the lease of Kiaochow Bay, close to the British-leased naval base of Weihaiwei — and the catalyst was the murder of two Roman Catholic German missionaries. In addition, the French leased Kwangchow Bay, southwest of Hong Kong, and the British extended the border of the latter to encompass the lease of the New Territories.

Defeat by Japan spurred the activities of reformers, and in the spring of 1898 the Emperor seemed to take courage and to rally to their cause.

THE HUNDRED DAYS OF REFORM

FLANKED BY TZ'U-HSI'S SPIES AND THE ARCH CONSERVATIVES OF THE IMPERIAL COURT, THE YOUNG EMPEROR, in his mid-twenties, had little chance to sense the infectious excitement that was coursing through the minds of young reformers within his empire. Memorials calling for reform were received in the palace, but were countered by the strident rejection of change from traditionalists.

Emperor Kuang-hsu had always known the power of the conservatives, for their opposition to his succession — which broke the laws laid down by previous dynasties — had festered through his early years on the Dragon Throne. And when China's first minister visited Britain, the conservative literati — refusing to acknowledge that the empire had anything to learn from the West — had cruelly satirized him. When he later wrote with admiration of the history of Western civilization, his claims were denounced and the printing blocks on which his heresy was written were destroyed.

However, arsenals and dockyards, railways and telegraph lines, mines and textile mills, and the establishment of "government-supervised merchant undertakings" such as the China Merchants' Steam Navigation Company, were transforming the face of the empire. And the reform movement was campaigning for change in a whole range of areas — from the abolition of foot-binding (which was prohibited to Manchu women, but was widely practised by all but peasant Chinese) to the jettisoning of the "eight-legged essay", mainstay of the outmoded public examination system.

"Chinese culture for foundation, Western learning for practical application" became the philosophy of

reformers such as the Confucian scholar K'ang Yu-wei who petitioned the young Emperor to lead the reform movement in his famous Letter of Ten Thousand Words. But whereas K'ang was a supporter of the dynasty and many of the traditions that were the foundations of the ancient civilization, his fiery colleague T'an Ssu-t'ung saw that grafting military and mercantile practises onto a Confucian, agrarian society would not bring about the revolutionary changes he envisaged. T'an was looking beyond the telegraph lines, trains, guns and mills to what he saw as the foundations of real change: the adoption of legal systems and political institutions of the West that would produce a new China able to regain its dignity and sovereignty.

When Tz'u-hsi suspected that her nephew — who had languished ineffectively in the luxury of his court — was imbibing the revolutionary zeal of the reformers, she immediately dismissed his reform-minded tutor, Weng T'ung-ho. But the bond between Kuang-hsu and his mentor persisted and when her spies informed her that the tutor was relaying the movement's ambitions to the young Emperor, she banished the tutor from the Forbidden City.

The railway link was an important event that brought many high-ranking Chinese officials to the colony during Governor Lugard's term of office.

The rhetoric of the reform movement, however, had already permeated the maze of walls within walls that sealed Emperor Kuang-hsu from his subjects. The seeds of interest had been sown when he had read K'ang's Letter of Ten Thousand Words in 1895 — the year in which China suffered its most humiliating defeat at the hands of the "dwarf barbarians". Now, three years later, they would briefly blossom.

"Do not the foreign Powers surround our Empire, committing frequent acts of aggression? Unless we learn and adopt the sources of their strength, our plight cannot be remedied," wrote the Emperor in 1898.

When Emperor Kuang-hsu and the reformer K'ang met during the spring of 1898, a spate of important decrees followed in what was later dubbed the heady Hundred Days of the Reform Movement. As if to proclaim the dawning of a new era, the reforms touched all sections of society. The education system was to be reorganized, with schools being established in the provinces and a university in Peking. There were reforms to the army and navy. Sinecures were to be abolished. A chamber of commerce and new government departments were to be established. And the building of railways and the establishment of industries were to be encouraged.

Predictably a howl of outrage followed from those who had much to lose from the reforms, and the criticism of conservatives was channelled to the Summer Palace, to Tz'u-hsi.

The Empress Dowager summoned the young Emperor, warning him that her long-time supporter,

Jung-lu, was in command of some one hundred thousand metropolitan troops. She also forbade the Emperor from ever again contacting the reformer K'ang Yu-wei.

Isolated within the Forbidden City, the Emperor sent a note to K'ang and T'an telling them of the Empress Dowager's anger and appealing to them for help.

The reformers rashly approached a soldier who had expressed support for the reform movement. Yuan Shih-k'ai was a distinguished military commander but one primarily interested in his own advancement. When the reformers invited him to participate in a daring plan to imprison the Empress Dowager (whose presence would always stifle reform) and to kill Jung-lu, Yuan played along with them, while informing Jung-lu, his superior officer, of the plot.

In no time at all the outraged Empress Dowager had confronted the bewildered Emperor, had banished him to an island prison on one of the lotus-covered lakes in the imperial city, and had issued an abdication in his name, stating: "From this day forth her Majesty will transact the business of the government..."

The reformers were pursued with vengeance. K'ang eluded capture — with help from the British — and escaped to Japan where he continued to campaign for reform. However, T'an, along with five others who became the martyred "Six Gentlemen of the Reform Movement", were executed.

As T'an, the thirty-three-year-old revolutionary, bared his neck to the sword, his words were guaranteed to fire the spirit of his followers: "I am willing to shed my blood, if thereby my country may be saved. But for everyone that perishes today, a thousand will rise up to carry on the work of Reform..."

Left: **English teacher and pupils at Peking University.** *Top:* **The education system was reorganized with books and schools being made accessible in China's far-flung provinces.**
Above: **The warlord Zhang Zoulin with his son Zhang Xueliang (right) who in his later years kidnapped Chiang Kai-shek in the "Sian Incident".**

THE FISTS OF RIGHTEOUS HARMONY

AS THE 20TH CENTURY DAWNED, THE EMPRESS DOWAGER PRESIDED OVER A CHINA VERY DIFFERENT FROM THAT visited by Lord Macartney more than a century earlier.

Foreign buildings, looking much as if they had been plucked from Europe, rose on the waterfronts of treaty ports where both Chinese and foreign merchants traded. Within the solid walls of ancient Chinese cities, the spires and façades of cathedrals rose amid the ornamental rooftops of Chinese temples. The imperial army was being drilled and equipped on Western lines and the empire's entire customs service — raising about a third of the government's revenue — was run by the dapper Irishman, Sir Robert Hart, who was loyal to both Queen

Victoria and the Empress Dowager, and had been honoured by both. Chinese students studied at mission schools and colleges within the treaty ports, using them as stepping stones for further studies abroad.

Steamships plied the inland waterways, railways snaked through the countryside and telegraph wires linked major cities. And, within the first few weeks of 1900, they carried to the foreigners — in the capital and treaty ports — disturbing news of an anti-foreign movement that had been ignited in the northern provinces, but was moving towards the capital. The movement apparently had the covert support of the Empress Dowager.

Tz'u-hsi was simmering with resentment at the fact that the foreign powers had let it be known they would react strongly should any unfortunate "accident" befall her unfilial nephew. In addition, the English had intervened to secure the release of a troublesome young revolutionary, Dr Sun Yat-sen, who had been kidnapped by her officials in London with the intention of bringing him home to certain execution. The British had also helped the traitorous reformer K'ang to escape to Japan where he continued to champion reform.

Since resuming the reins of power, the Empress Dowager had adopted a resolute stance in the face of the

The Australian Mission in Peking.

multiplicity of foreign demands — for land, mining and railway concessions. She flatly refused an Italian demand for a naval base, and declared there would be no more railway lines. The latter was a source of enormous local resentment, for the iron-wheeled wagons had stolen the livelihood of muleteers, porters and boatmen. In addition, the metal tracks disturbed the harmony of the earth's spirits — feng shui — just as surely as the foreign telegraph lines and mine shafts.

The final years of the 19th century had convinced the Empress Dowager that appeasement had been equated with weakness by the foreign powers, and military "self-strengthening" (the only one of her nephew's reforms she had not abolished) had not yet equipped her empire with the requisite power to repel foreign aggression.

The extravagance of her own court and the financial burden of war indemnities were edging China closer to bankruptcy — and when famine and floods added to the empire's calamities, Tz'u-hsi pinned her hopes on magic.

The source of the magic was a fast-growing brotherhood of fanatical young men who tied blood-red bands around their heads and waists, and whipped themselves into an entranced frenzy of spirit boxing and incantation. Surrounding foreign churches and homes, and forcing onlookers to kneel and chant, their shouts of "Burn, burn, burn! Kill, kill, kill!" would become chillingly familiar to foreigners during the summer of 1900.

The festering threat of malcontents was nothing new in China. Rebellion had become as predictable as the flooding of turbulent rivers — particularly when officials pocketed the money assigned for embankment repairs.

Thus, in the spring of 1900, the secret society dubbed "the Boxers" — its name translated as "the Fists of Righteous Harmony" — lured many, as had the martial call of the Taipings forty years earlier.

There were unemployed soldiers; undernourished peasants who had lost crops to drought, locusts or floods; anti-Manchu elements that were tamed when the Empress Dowager indicated support for the movement; and xenophobic officials only too delighted to support the angry young men whose fantastic antics alarmed the nations vying over the vivisection of China.

And, at the core of the movement, was the widespread, deep-seated resentment aroused by missionaries who boldly carried their faiths to far corners of the empire, assuming they would supplant the blend of beliefs that had served the people for so long.

The missionaries' conviction of the superiority of their faiths was affront enough, but when Roman Catholic cathedrals rose on sites that had accommodated temples, and bishops demanded (and received) the rank and privileges of viceroys — parading through the streets with ceremonial umbrellas and a retinue of attendants — officials, local priests and the people were outraged.

The missionaries also made enemies of local magistrates by interfering in court cases involving converts by demanding that they receive special treatment. As some of the professed converts were of dubious character and clearly fell into the category of "rice Christians" ("You eat Jesus's rice, you speak his words"), the magistrates bitterly resented the undermining of their authority.

Missionary orphanages also aroused suspicion, for they paid those who brought them the babies abandoned on the streets each night. They intended to baptise even the dying, but there was dark speculation about their motives, and the practice of "buying" abandoned children had resulted in kidnappings. Already anti-missionary riots in Tientsin in 1870 had claimed the lives of several French Sisters of Charity who ran an orphanage. The imposing French cathedral — built on the site of a Chinese temple — was burnt to the ground by an angry mob.

Fantastic tales about the power of alien faiths were spun by those that wished to fan resentment against missionary societies. Although they could claim few genuine converts, the societies often provided services appreciated by locals, such as medical aid, schooling and printing presses. Their good deeds were clearly resented by those — such as herbalists or scholars — who saw their own skills or authority threatened.

It had not escaped the notice of the Manchu gentry in Peking that the revolutionary movements gathering strength in the south were invariably led by mission-educated idealists, such as the young Hong Kong trained doctor and revolutionary, Sun Yat-sen. And that Sun's political activities were financed by the wealthy Methodist-educated businessman Charlie Soong who returned to Shanghai as an ordained minister in 1886, then went into business. Soong did much to rally both overseas and local support for Sun, who would later marry one of his daughters.

But when the Boxers first began to emerge as a serious problem, Charlie Soong's daughter, Ching-ling, had not yet been born and Dr Sun was evading Ch'ing authorities. Following his first failed attempt at a revolutionary uprising in 1885, there was a price of one thousand silver dollars on his head.

With political unrest and financial and natural disasters mounting, Boxer pamphlets and posters were soon laying the blame for all the woes of the nation on the foreigners and, in particular, the missionaries.

"The scandalous conduct of Christians and barbarians is angering our gods and spirits, hence the many scourges from which we are now suffering. The dreadful drought afflicting vast areas this year will continue as long as one single Western Devil resides within the Four Seas," read one Boxer poster.

"The iron roads and carriages are disturbing the terrestrial dragon and destroying the earth's beneficial influences," ran another.

"The unfortunate people attending religious services are being bewitched," claimed a third. "As for children received in orphanages, they are killed and their intestines are used to change lead into silver and make precious remedies."

The Empress Dowager was naturally happy to deflect the people's anger away from the failures of her own dynasty. Though she had never seen the Boxers in action, she was excited by reports relayed by her Chief Eunuch. He told of the supernatural powers of red-turbaned young heroes, who cut the air with their

swords; of bullets that did not wound the invulnerable Boxers; and of spectacles that drew people into the dusty town squares where the Boxers practised their martial arts.

China's ancient skepticism had always been tempted by the promise of the supernatural. Could the Boxers deliver China from its ever-worsening situation or were they, as claimed, merely engaging in theatrical chicanery with blank cartridges and blunt swords? Could the red-turbaned youth that the Governor of Shantung, Yuan Shih-k'ai, set before his firing squads have been real Boxers or merely troublemakers masquerading?

The Empress Dowager even entertained the notion that the fanatical Boxers might infuse her entire nation with their zeal. Even her trusted military commander Jung-lu admired their spirit and willingness to die for their cause.

And so when in a single day in 1900, in the courtyard of the governor's residence in Shansi, some forty-five missionaries — men, women and children — were decapitated, Tz'u-hsi would later commend the governor responsible for ridding his province of "a whole brood of foreign devils".

*Left: **Ancient pagoda and the spires of Canton Cathedral — spiritual symbols of East and West.***
*Top: **Mrs McMullan and her Chinese orphans at the Australian Mission.***

$\mathcal{W}$hile Tz'u-hsi applauded the Shansi massacre, she vacillated before giving official support to the Boxer movement.

Soon the Boxers began to multiply in the capital, prompting Dr George Morrison, correspondent of The Times of London, to sense peril in the air and to observe that all knives and swords had doubled in value, and shops were working day and night to supply the demand for weapons.

Initially members of the foreign legations in Peking had considered reports filtering into the capital to be exaggerated. So Queen Victoria's eighty-first (and last) birthday was celebrated in May with champagne, toasts and dancing on the decorated tennis court of the British Legation to "I.G's Own" — the brass band established by the Inspector General of Chinese Customs, Sir Robert Hart.

But as the heat of summer mounted, nerves within legation complexes began to fray. The reports — and the increasing presence of the Boxers within the capital — became impossible to ignore.

Reinforcements were called by the foreign ministers in Peking, but an international force which set out from the treaty port of Tientsin was driven back by the Boxer brotherhood, backed now by Imperial troops.

Tz'u-hsi was increasingly showing her hand and, ignoring the advice of moderates, was giving the virulently anti-foreign Prince Tuan, father of the heir apparent, the authority to mount what he hoped would be a massacre of foreigners.

When the Chancellor of the Japanese Legation, impeccably attired in a bowler hat and tail coat, was hacked to death as he prepared to meet the requested reinforcements at the railway station, and within days a Manchu soldier had shot the German Minister, Baron von Ketteler, at point-blank range, the terrified foreigners took refuge in the barricaded legation quarters. Hastily they prepared for one of the most extraordinary sieges in history.

As the butchery of Christian converts and foreigners mounted, and bands of chanting Boxers closed in on the legation quarters, the Empress Dowager issued a decree declaring that China was at war with Great Britain, the United States, Germany, France, Italy, Austria, Belgium, Holland and Japan.

On the first day of the now declared war, the elated Prince Tuan was able to report the rapid retreat of foreigners from not only Sir Robert Hart's customs building, but the Belgian, Dutch, Austro-Hungarian, Italian and

French legations. It wasn't long before he added that the Germans and Americans had been forced to abandon a particularly strategic outpost they had held on the city walls.

The entire foreign community was now penned within the British Legation and a series of timber buildings set in adjacent gardens. "The foreigners," pro-nounced Tz'u-hsi, "are like fish in a stew pan." It became a matter of whether to shoot them out, or to torch the timber buildings and smoke them out.

Either way, Prince Tuan and the Empress Dowager considered them as easy prey as the four thousand converts, twenty-two nuns and a handful of French sailors who were trying to withstand an assault on the Northern Cathedral. All they had was a single cannon, the prayers of the French Bishop and the bravery of a young Breton sailor whose memory would linger well beyond his short life.

The British Legation had been the obvious point of retreat because it was the least exposed of the legation buildings. Set within a three-acre compound that normally accommodated sixty people, it soon held the entire foreign community of Peking — diplomats and customs officials, mining and railway engineers, soldiers and missionaries.

In all there were some five hundred civilians, a garrison of over four hundred officers and men, plus more than two thousand Chinese converts and several hundred Chinese who had been employed in foreign households and offices.

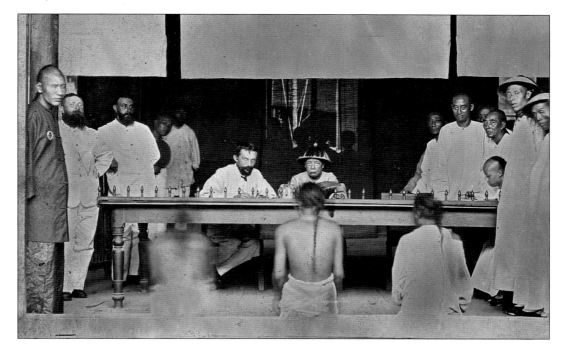

While the Boxers boasted an extraordinary array of weapons, from double-edged broadswords to rifles, and the imperial army had recently taken delivery of some impressive nine-pounders from Baron Krupp's German factory, the defenders had only four pieces of light artillery and limited ammunition.

Little wonder the French Minister wrung his hands ("Nous sommes perdus!") while a German resident, who shared his foreboding, played Wagner on the piano.

With the brisk efficiency that was the hallmark of colonial bureaucracies, the British Minister, Sir Claude MacDonald, set about coordinating the defence of his multinational guests. Quite often his orders were issued on his gilt-edged diplomatic cards.

Committees mushroomed to deal with every aspect of seige life, from sanitation to sorties to secure

Top left: **Dr George Morrison, correspondent for The Times of London.** *Left:* **Count Waldersee, Commander-in-Chief of Allied Forces.** *Above:* **Boxer trial following the uprising.**

armaments and ammunition. The women rapidly turned the legation's damask curtains into sandbags that added a bizarre carnival gaiety to the barricades. Long lines of diplomatic wives and children put out intermittant fires by passing water containers — chamber pots, vases, pitchers — hand-to-hand. Chinese converts did much of the heavy work — digging trenches, strengthening barricades — and somehow survived on meagre rations.

Once initial food stocks had disappeared, magpies and sparrows were bagged, and the cooks tried variations on the staple of horseflesh and rice as one by one some one hundred and fifty prized racing and hunting ponies met an untimely end. Despite the less-than-tempting fare, the Marquis di Salvago Raggi, the Italian Minister, insisted on dressing for dinner each night.

During lulls in the fighting, the English predictably played cricket; the Swiss proprietor of the Hotel de Pekin and his young American wife produced several hundred loaves a day while shells demolished the walls of their hotel; and the American Polly Condit Smith, one of a summer party rescued from the Western Hills by the adventurous correspondent for The Times, declared Dr George Morrison to be the most attractive man in their impromptu mess. Morrison, an Australian doctor, had in fact been largely responsible for the rescue of many of the Chinese converts who crowded the legation complex.

When the Boxers set fire to the triple-tiered gateway to the Tatar City, destroying some of the city's best-known antique, jewellery and fur stores, Tz'u-hsi may well have suspected that they were out of control and that, as Yuan Shih-k'ai had warned, they were merely murderers and looters. However, she continued to vacillate. Certainly her loyal Jung-lu considered the seige "a piece of stupidity which would be remembered against China

for all time." And the fact that the imperial army's nine-pounders saw little action during the seige said much for his military restraint.

Tz'u-hsi was also aware that her edicts ordering hostilities against foreigners throughout the empire were being ignored in provinces where moderates, such as Li Hung-chang and Yuan Shih-k'ai, continued to deal harshly with the Boxers, pay back foreign war indemnities and reassure treaty port residents that the uprising would be contained around the capital.

As June stretched into July, and there was still no sign of the long-awaited international relief force, foreign frustration and fear mounted along with the soaring temperatures of summer. As telegraph lines out of the city had been cut since mid-June, the outside world now held little hope for Peking's foreign community. Sir Robert Hart's last message to Tientsin had read: "Foreign community beseiged in the legations. Situation desperate. Make haste!"

In mid-July, the London Daily Mail carried a report the world had been expecting: the seige was over; the spirited defenders of the legation had been massacred.

"Standing together as the sun rose fully, the little remaining band, all Europeans, met death stubbornly. The Chinese lost heavily, but as one man fell, others advanced, and, finally, overcome by overwhelming odds, every one of the Europeans remaining was put to the sword in the most atrocious manner," claimed The Daily Mail on 16th July 1900.

Even The Times, not having heard from its resourceful correspondent, assumed his demise and wrote warmly of the doctor's life of high adventure: "Dr Morrison has had so many hairbreadth escapes in the course of his most adventurous life... that we cannot quite relinquish the hope that he may possibly have escaped in the confusion of the final slaughter."

A month later, when the relief force of twenty thousand troops finally arrived in Peking, it found a devastated city being abandoned by thousands of fleeing residents. But within the legation compound, the seige's survivors were in remarkably good shape.

During the fifty-five-day seige sixty-six foreigners had been killed and one hundred and fifty wounded. No one kept count of casualties among the Chinese converts. In the excitement of raising the seige, the predicament of those penned in the Northern Cathedral was overlooked, until a contingent of Japanese troops rescued the nuns and Chinese converts. They had endured an even more harrowing ordeal and owed their lives to a gallant Breton sailor, who had stolen an imperial cannon to defend them. He had died two weeks before the troops arrived.

It was abundantly clear to the rescuers that, in making their brave and resourceful stand, the foreign community had not dropped its standards. The dusty troops noted with astonishment the finery of some of the women and the starched collars of diplomats not engaged in fighting. It surprised them not at all to hear that, during a lull in fighting, the dapper Sir Robert Hart had thrown a letter addressed to his London tailor over the wall to a courier. "Send quickly two autumn suits and later two winter ditto with morning and evening dress,"

Survivors of the legation seige.

it instructed. "I have lost everything but am well. Hart, Peking." The warm clothing duly arrived two months later.

When the emotional scenes of the rescue were over and the beseiged prepared to leave their makeshift accommodation, foreign troops were already heading for the Forbidden City — and the treasure they knew it must hold.

"Peking is now entirely under foreign control. Looting is proceeding systematically. ...The Dowager Empress, the Emperor, Prince Tuan and all the high officers have escaped. ...There is no Government," read Dr George Morrison's telegraph to The Times on 17th August 1900.

When she heard the muffled roar of the foreign Maxim guns and anticipated the orgy of rape and reprisal that would accompany victory, Tz'u-hsi hastily gathered a small retinue.

She already knew that the city's wells were choked with the bodies of women; that countless officials, soldiers and residents had committed suicide rather than face the latest humiliation at the hand of the foreign powers. Later she would put around a story that she herself had sought this honourable alternative to flight, but that her ministers had forced her to abandon a chosen spot "where bullets fell like rain and where the enemy's guns gathered thick as forest trees."

As the tenor of panic — of terrified eunuchs and wailing concubines — rose against the deep throb of the advancing guns, the sixty-five-year-old Empress Dowager instinctively sought the sanctuary of her ancestral homeland. She needed to put the formidable Great Wall between her and the allied armies who would seek to make her capture a crowning glory to their victory.

Already a great river of humanity streamed from the capital — and Tz'u-hsi joined it.

Gone were the pearl embroidered Manchu slippers, the jade sheaths that protected her six-inch-long nails, the jewelled headdresses. Now her hair was knotted in a bun and she wore the blue cotton homespun of the peasants who surrounded her with the shrill panic of flight.

With her was the Emperor, grieving over the loss of the Pearl Concubine. As the group prepared to leave the palace, the spirited concubine had pleaded against the undignified flight — evoking memories of Tz'u-hsi's appeal when Emperor Hsien-feng had abandoned his capital in 1860. The Empress Dowager hesitated just long enough to order her eunuchs to cast her nephew's favourite into a palace well and instruct her Chief Eunuch to bury her prized possessions.

Initially she headed north, but the Boxers had been active in several Manchurian provinces and the Russians were busy establishing a protectorate over the troubled provinces. So the party turned south and made for the ancient T'ang dynasty capital of Sian in Shensi.

When Tz'u-hsi had the leisure to gather her thoughts, savour a water pipe, and dispatch her retainers to gather tribute, she knew that, with the shreds of power left to her, she must expunge from the records anything that revealed her support for the Boxers.

Princes of the blood and ministers who had urged her along that path would have to be offered the silken cord with which to commit suicide, or be banished — as was Prince Tuan — to Turkestan. She did not want witnesses to her rash lapse of judgement.

And when, to her surprise, the allies did not pursue her and seemed content with their looting and some punitive raids on towns where Boxer atrocities had occurred, she prepared to return to her capital.

More than a year after her flight from Peking, the cavalcade of the imperial procession appeared at the gate of the Tatar City. Tz'u-hsi alighted from a sedan trimmed with peacock feathers to acknowledge the Emperor's ceremonial gesture of welcome as he knelt before her.

She had waived the rule which prevented foreigners from viewing the Emperor and, catching sight of a group of foreigners who had gathered on the city walls — not far from the spot where a bitter seige battle had occurred — the symbolism of the moment was not lost on the ageing Empress Dowager.

Surrounded by the panoply of banners and palanquins, of cavalry, eunuchs and officials, the empress pressed her hands together beneath her chin in a traditional greeting, and made a series of small bows.

It was a gesture that acknowledged much had changed, and its charm illicited a surprising burst of applause from the foreigners who sought a glimpse of the woman who had plotted their massacre.

Soon representatives of the powers had resumed their rivalry for China's favours and were squabbling over railway and mining rights, while their wives were being lavishly entertained by the diminutive and charming empress in the Forbidden City.

In newly-furnished palace apartments that had been plundered by soldiers and diplomats alike — a British officer noted that Lady MacDonald, wife of the British Minister, had "devoted herself most earnestly to looting" — the empress passed around American cigarettes, served champagne and graciously apologized for being unable to present her guests with one of the famous Pekingese dogs bred in her palace stables. Unfortunately, she lamented in her melodious voice, the Boxers had killed them all.

*Left: **The Bronze Temple in the Summer Palace.***
*Above: **The Empress Dowager entertains the wives of foreign diplomats.***

THE BIRTH OF REPUBLICAN CHINA

WHEN TZ'U-HSI HAD GONE WITHOUT FOOD DURING HER FLIGHT FROM THE CAPITAL, SHE WITNESSED, FOR THE first time in her life, the grim treadmill of poverty that defined the lives of the vast majority of her subjects.

Restored to the luxury of the Forbidden City, she did not forget her experience and in January 1901 issued an edict that revived many of the reforms originally initiated by her nephew. Tz'u-hsi's instinct for survival had been sharpened by the near collapse of her dynasty. She had noted the rumblings of revolution in the always troublesome south, and the rising power of Chinese viceroys such as Li Hung-chang and Yuan Shih-k'ai whose provinces had simply ignored her Boxer edicts.

She may also have appreciated that her restoration to power had less to do with the strength of her dynasty's mandate than the fact that neither the republicans in the south nor the reformers in exile in Japan had the requisite power to govern China.

There had been talk among the victorious powers of partitioning China, but rising tensions between them were such that gunfire had been exchanged during their occupation of Peking. Negotiating an official carve-up of the failing eastern empire would have been a time-consuming feat — and everyone wanted to get back to business. Eventually they followed the advice of Sir Robert Hart and those who urged support for the dynasty.

Before she had fled the capital, the Empress Dowager had summoned Li Hung-chang, China's elder statesman, to negotiate yet another peace agreement with the foreigners. The seventy-seven-year-old Li, frail, white-bearded and partially paralyzed, might have been a symbol of the dynasty he had served. Servants helped him to the negotiating table and for the last time he set his seal to an agreement which further exacerbated the economic woes and military standing of the empire: China was to pay a sixty-seven million pound war indemnity; it was not to rebuild the Taku forts; it was not to import arms.

"China's position was worse than a colony," lamented the revolutionary leader, Dr Sun Yat-sen. "She was at the mercy of the powers, yet there was not one paternalistic colonial power to whom she could turn for mercy."

Top right: **Yuan Shih-k'ai, the military commander who betrayed the young Emperor and became President of the Republic.** *Right:* **Protestors at Peking University.**

Shortly after he signed the Boxer Protocol, Li collapsed and died. He had presided over the empire's foreign affairs for decades, had vigorously urged China down the road of "self-strengthening", and had exploited every opportunity to reap financial rewards for himself from business interests that ranged from fancy stores and money brokerage firms in Nanking and Shanghai to shipping, banking and mining. A weakness for nepotism and the douceurs offered when negotiating concessions had assured him a notorious reputation among diplomats, and the eventual contempt of many of his countrymen.

Tz'u-hsi's apparent change of heart towards reform was greeted with scepticism by her subjects. To revolutionaries, it was too little too late; to conservative officials, it was anathema — and would be resisted; to more enlightened officials, there was doubt and confusion. They were haunted by the memory of reprisals against officials who had promptly implemented her nephew's reforms during the Hundred Days of the Reform

Movement. It was whispered that Tz'u-hsi did not truly support reform. They likened her reform edicts to her rewriting of history, seeing in them a duplicity they had come to know during her many decades in power.

And so, in the aftermath of the rebellion, the pace of unrest quickened. The anti-foreign stance of the rebellion had harboured a patriotic element now evident in the growing membership of secret societies intent on forging a new China. Dr Sun Yat-sen, son of poor peasants from the south, was initially seen as a disloyal rebel. Now he was viewed as a high-minded patriot and support for the revolution he advocated grew from all echelons of society.

*I*n the 20th century China would absorb more change in the first few decades than it had known in centuries preceding the twilight of its empire. And the death within the century's first decade of both the Emperor and the Empress Dowager hastened the course of change.

The Emperor's health had been failing for several years and on 14th November 1908, he died. At that time Tz'u-hsi was plagued by dysentery. A day after the Emperor's death, a favourite dish of clotted cream and crab apples became her last indulgence. In her deathbed valedication, she observed: "Looking back upon the memories of these last fifty years, I perceive how calamities from within and aggression from without have come upon us in relentless succession, and that my life has never enjoyed a moment's respite from anxiety."

The deaths inevitably stirred rumours in the teahouses — that the Empress Dowager had engineered her nephew's death, or that Yuan Shih-k'ai had conspired to ensure that the Emperor he had betrayed did not outlive the woman whose power he had protected.

Before dying, Tz'u-hsi appointed the last Emperor, the two-year-old P'u Yi, heir to the Dragon Throne. The new Emperor's mother was Jung-lu's daughter.

Beyond the Forbidden City the tide of revolution was rising. Several unsuccessful uprisings had already claimed lives, creating martyrs and strengthening the resolve of their followers.

Finally, in October 1911, an eleventh attempt at revolution — prematurely triggered by the unscheduled explosion of a hidden arsenal in the Russian concession of Hankow — gathered a momentum that the Ch'ing dynasty found impossible to halt.

Suddenly the streets were filled with revolutionaries, determined to shed the outworn mantle of an ancient and unyielding civilization. One by one China's provinces declared themselves for the republic.

The revolutionaries had garnered their political philosophies and social ideals from a handful of Western

Communist troops enter Peking, restored as the capital with the birth of the People's Republic of China.

nations that — despite their rivalries and territorial ambitions — had opened China's eyes to a wider world through the treaty ports that laced the coastline.

Within the ports protected by extraterritoriality, revolutionaries — immune to the jurisdiction of Manchu China — had been able to exchange ideas with English intellectuals, Russian revolutionaries and French socialists; had printed revolutionary pamphlets; and plotted the overthrow of the House of Ch'ing.

Manchu resistance to the revolution quickly crumbled, and in December 1911 Dr Sun Yat-sen was declared the first provisional president of the Republic of China. Within weeks, the boy Emperor and the widowed dowager — the late Emperor's Lustrous Concubine — abdicated, bringing to an end two hundred and sixty-eight years of Manchu rule and an empire that had existed for two thousand years.

"It is not fitting that we should withstand the desires of the nation merely for the glorification of Our House," read the abdication edict issued in February 1912. "We recognize the signs of the ages... and decree the establishment of a constitutional government on a republican basis."

The republicans magnanimously agreed that P'u Yi could retain his title, his household in the Forbidden City and a generous annual subsidy. But in sidelining the symbols of imperial power, they were preserved and would later be exploited.

However, in the euphoria of the republic's birth, the notion of restoring the bad old days of imperial rule seemed unthinkable. China was a cauldron of energy and idealism centred on the dream of building a new

nation — and changes were immediately apparent on the streets. Almost overnight the queue, for so long the symbol of submission to Manchu rule, disappeared to be replaced by short haircuts and Western-style hats or caps. The retention of the queue became a political statement, and when attempts were later made to restore the empire, barbers did a great trade in false queues for a confused public.

As men shed their queues, women shed the bandages binding their feet in a centuries-old practice that produced both tiny feet and the mincing, swaying gait of the well-to-do woman. Designed to create the "golden lily" feet that men found so enticing, the practice of foot-binding was roundly condemned by Western women when first encountered in China. Only peasant women — unable to afford the loss of mobility — and Manchu women, forbidden to practise it, had escaped this crippling custom.

When they assumed control of the country, Dr Sun Yat-sen and his fellow republicans had a long list of admirable reforms that would turn China into a more egalitarian society. Democracy, land reform and a social revolution were high on the agenda, but to put such reforms into place required stability — and the nation was in ferment!

The untried political institutions of the fledgling republic were in the hands of politically inexperienced revolutionaries. The traditional social hierarchy was vanishing; the bureaucratic foundations that had long provided cohesion were shifting; and social patterns and traditions were being rapidly abandoned.

And what was more, China's streets were filled with impatient, young political activists, its countryside was awash with arms — most of them in the hands of restless, unpaid soldiers.

The situation was ripe for anarchy — or the seizure of power by warlords who had plagued the empire in the past and would care little for what they considered the impractical idealism of 20th-century republicans.

Appreciating the need for stability, Sun surrendered his presidency to the one man everyone was convinced would restore order: the former provincial governor and military commander, Yuan Shih-k'ai — who had supported the reform movement, then betrayed it.

Yuan, who won considerable standing after distinguishing himself militarily, had cleverly played republican against monarchist in his bid for the presidency. Now, with one million men under arms — twice as many as in Manchu China prior to the revolution — he used his military strength to emasculate the newly created National Assembly. He then resorted to tactics familiar to him — assassination, intimidation and bribery — to achieve dictatorial powers.

Although the new president appointed an array of foreign advisers — including Dr George Morrison, of The Times of London — he seldom consulted them. Soon a frustrated Morrison was recording: "There is probably more suffering in China at the present moment than there is in the whole of the rest of the world. China has created a force of armed brigands which she can no longer control."

Yuan did not even convey to his foreign advisers the contents of the notorious "Twenty-one Demands" presented to China by its increasingly aggressive neighbour.

Since it had claimed victory in the Russo-Japanese War of 1905, Japan had become a major contender in

the territorial chess game being played out in China. Having regained control of the strategic Liaotung Peninsula (which it had relinquished after the signing of the Treaty of Shimonoseki, only to see it fall into Russian hands), Japan now confidently took its place as a member of the imperial club. Britain was its ally and although it could not match the former in terms of territory (Britain had added over three million square miles to her empire in the last two decades of the 19th century), its victory demonstrated to the world that the Japanese army and navy could take on any European power.

While the powers considered the Russo-Japanese War a brutal little conflict on the edge of the world in which the machine gun made its debut — first in the hands of the Russians, then deployed with devastating effect by the Japanese — it radically altered the balance of power. It was not long before Japan consolidated its gains.

Seizing Nanking Station. The Japanese capture of the capital in 1937 saw the slaughter of some one hundred thousand residents.

It carefully timed the delivery of its "Twenty-one Demands". The foreign powers were engaged in World War I and China was racked by internal strife when in 1915 Japan issued its ultimatum, seeking to extend its control over Manchuria, Mongolia and the province of Shantung, seized from German control. Japan's demands would have reduced China to the state of a vassal and clearly revealed its long-term aim to dominate China. Yuan finally agreed to an amended ultimatum, setting off a wave of anti-Japanese protests.

When Japan had defeated Russia, it became an inspiration to Chinese students eager that their country should cast off the humiliating semi-colonial status imposed by Western powers. Now many disillusioned students abandoned the country that had served as their model and to which they had flocked to study. They gave vent to their indignation in anti-Japanese marches that were followed by strikes and boycotts of a range of Japanese goods and services — from cosmetics to brothels.

When, hard on the heels of this humiliation, Yuan revealed his own agenda for China — the restoration of imperial rule — revolution erupted once again. But Yuan's dream of becoming China's new emperor foundered, his supporters and henchmen deserted him and he died, in shame, in June 1916.

The nation now plunged headlong into a long, dark decade of lawlessness that Morrison had predicted and Yuan had unleashed. Increasingly there was division between warlords who seized power in the north — and were sometimes assisted by foreign loans — and the republicans who had established themselves firmly in the south.

The end of the war in Europe — in which some two hundred thousand Chinese coolies dug trenches and laboured on construction projects to release allied soldiers for the front — stirred high hopes in China. The republic's delegates at the peace talks in France during 1919 urged the return of territories originally seized or leased by Germany, and since taken over by Japan. But at the Versailles Peace Conference, reciprocal deals were done between the allies, and Japan emerged triumphant — with the same imperial privileges previously enjoyed by Germany. When Britain, France and the United States upheld Japan's claims in China, their action sparked a sense of betrayal and disillusion akin to that of Japan's "Twenty-one Demands".

Peking University, already a hotbed of political radicalism, became the focus for a May demonstration of five thousand protestors that historians would later hail as the first mass movement in China's modern history.

Nationalist leader Chiang Kai-shek and Communist leader Mao Tse-tung.

The May the Fourth Movement expressed the nation's sense of outrage and disillusion. It called for a rethinking of the way ahead.

Some of those who gathered outside the university continued to pursue the dream of Western democracy; others turned to Russia and the revolutionary doctrines that fired its radical leadership. Mao Tse-tung, an assistant librarian at Peking University, began to imbibe the Marxism that had been studied at the university since the previous year. He would later admit that at the time his mind was a "curious mixture of ideas — of liberalism, democratic reform and utopian socialism." All the political possibilities that excited students at the time.

The 1920s was a tumultuous decade for China — a decade of intense ideological ferment, of financial chaos, of civil conflict and warlord atrocities. Halfway through the decade, foreign loans to warlords had enabled them to amass huge armies and to bring the number of men under arms in China to one-and-a-half million — triple what it had been a decade earlier.

The decade began with the birth of the Communist Party in Shanghai's French Concession in 1921. It later witnessed a marriage of convenience between Sun's Nationalist Party and the Communists — an alliance fractured by mutual distrust which ended in a bloodbath in 1927 as Nationalist troops hunted down their former comrades and slaughtered them, by the thousands, in the streets.

In that same year, warlord troops in Peking massacred both Nationalist and Communist students mounting a peaceful protest against foreign influence in China. The troops opened fired on the protesters, then used their bayonets on the wounded. Later they robbed the bodies of the dead.

Western observers, such as the American scholar Sidney Gamble, chronicled and captured on camera the despair of this decade of turmoil. In 1926, he wrote of the arrival in Peking of thousands of wounded warlord troops, and the dearth of doctors and drugs in a city already swollen by refugees from famine. Countless died of cold and frostbite on the streets that winter.

Gamble also recorded how the soldiers made survival impossible for peasants who, with the first spring rains, prepared to return to their fields.

"In some places the horses of the army have been grazed in the wheat fields," he wrote. "From other villages we hear that the soldiers have demanded scythes so that they can cut the grain themselves. The soldiers have put signs on some wheat fields saying that the grain must not be disturbed as it is for their use. It looks very much as though the countryside would be faced with famine before fall."

But there were, of course, diversions.

In 1922 P'u Yi, the last Emperor, turned sixteen and Peking's winter streets were cleared of corpses so that everyone could enjoy the spectacle of his lavish champagne wedding. P'u Yi took not one but two brides — a Mongol beauty who quickly became addicted to drugs and a second consort who soon abandoned him. The teahouses were rife with speculation about P'u Yi's sexuality, for he sported the distinctive dark glasses so favoured by effeminate young apprentices being trained for female roles in Peking opera, who were the darlings of society at the time.

No one, however, questioned the sexuality of the starlets of the nation's new film industry, ravishingly photographed in masculine suits and trilby hats during those early years of feminism in the 1920s. Nor that of the

Manchu princess, who swaggered in Japanese military dress to illustrate the fact that her lover was the head of the Japanese secret service in Shanghai.

And when the nation's woes multiplied towards the end of the decade, everyone applauded the timely appearance of an inspired new fashion that adapted the high collars and side fastenings of the Manchu gowns being discarded by males — in a female version which barely covered the knees of the young beauties who flaunted it. Produced by Shanghai's ingenious tailors, the cheongsam perfectly captured the insouciant gaiety of that city on the eve of Depression.

By the end of the extraordinary decade, Chiang Kai-shek had succeeded Dr Sun Yat-sen and had subdued the northern warlords and united most of China under a Nationalist Government — but at a price. There had been little time to put into practice the promised reforms that had fuelled support for Sun's revolution.

Sun died a disappointed man in 1925, admonishing his followers that the revolution was far from complete. Not only was he disappointed in its outcome, but in the lack of support he had received from foreign nations with an economic stake in China. Two years before he died he told the New York Times that he had lost hope of securing support and aid from America, Britain or France. The only country that had supported China was Russia. "The prevailing estimate of Dr Sun is that he is a dreamer and therefore dangerous," observed the Times.

Although the dreamer's high ideals of "land to the tiller", economic reform and social revolution seemed stillborn under the leadership of the soldier Chiang Kai-shek, their promise was the basic creed of the Communist leader Mao Tse-tung whose followers were spreading it through the countryside. After the purge of the Communists in the cities, Mao concentrated his efforts on the eighty per cent of the population who lived off the land, under the heel of officials and landlords. To those living in mud-walled hovels where there was never enough food for children, the Communist creed became a holy doctrine — and one worth fighting for. By 1932 the Communists controlled much of the provinces of Honau and Kiangsi, and claimed the loyalty of some nine million followers.

Having defeated the warlords, Chiang, the new president of the republic, now turned his sights on his political rivals and by 1934 his military net was closing on the Communists. With the unified nation now witnessing the emergence of a middle class that enjoyed considerable affluence in cities such as Shanghai, Chiang saw the Communists as the enemy within, a cancer that had to be destroyed if stability was to be maintained. Eventually the Red Army sustained such heavy losses that its remnants embarked on an epic trek that would take them far beyond the well-equipped Nationalist Army.

The now legendary Long March initially involved some ninety thousand troops and followers. When the marchers arrived at their destination in northern Shensi they numbered only twenty thousand.

In the tawny hills and crisp dry air of Yenan, the Communists established a new base, living in caves and working in headquarters that had paper windows and bamboo furniture. The Eighth Route Army grew its own food, women spun and sewed the cloth for their uniforms, and guerrilla bands were trained so that,

when the time was right, they could group together to form a formidable force. Recruits received both military and political training. Mao Tse-tung told his followers: "Political power grows out of the barrel of a gun." But he knew that to use his weapon effectively and win victory, a man had to know what he was fighting for.

When China was not waging civil war in the 1930s, it was battling its ambitious neighbour. Young militarists had eclipsed civilian authority in Japan and coups and assassinations presaged the dark days of militarism to come. Encouraged by its easy conquest in Manchuria in 1932 — where it created the puppet state of Manchukuo with the dynasty's last Emperor, P'u Yi, on the throne of his ancestral homeland — Japan sought any pretext to occupy northern towns, as its troops began their relentless sweep through China.

In 1937, Nanking, the capital of the Nationalist Government, fell to the invaders and one hundred thousand civilians were butchered. The beseiged Chiang, refusing to surrender, moved his capital to a mountain fortress: Chungking. Salvaging what they could to carry to the provisional capital, troops and civilians endured a long and difficult journey into the mountains of Szechuan. Ringed by lofty peaks that were frequently enveloped with cloud, they were safe from attack by land, but exposed to the Japanese bombers that soon appeared on the horizon.

*Left: **Victorious Red Army troops enter Peking.** Above: **War ravaged streets as Nationalist troops flee Shanghai.***

On 3rd May 1939 — a night on which there was a total eclipse of the moon — Chungking endured a night of terror when twenty-seven Japanese bombers attacked the town at dusk. Its flimsy homes of wood and bamboo burnt easily; its streets were littered with casualties in this first ever mass bombing of a civilian population. When the attack was over, the night air was filled with the cries of the city, the fury of its fires — and the beat of gongs that sought to banish the dark shadow engulfing the moon.

Until the attack on Pearl Harbor in December 1941, China fought the Japanese juggernaut alone, and the heavy toll on the land and the people would scar the nation for years to come.

When the agony of the war years ended, a new international order had emerged. The age of colonialism was over. Foreign concessions were no more. China had regained its self-respect with the abolition of the unequal treaties that had cost it so much in territory and pride. It was the world's most populous nation and it took its rightful place as a member of the United Nations.

But there was still the unresolved conflict of the civil war between Nationalist and Communist — and the people were weary of war.

Above: **Communist forces enter Peking.**
Right: **The revolutionary leaders — Chairman Mao Tse-tung and Premier Chou En-lai.**

Physically and spiritually depleted by the war, the Nationalists tried to rally support, but when rampant post-war inflation destroyed the emerging middle class that was its power base, it was doomed.

America, now dominant in the Pacific, tried to bring the rival forces together, as it had during the war. But while an agreement appeared to have been reached — Chiang and Mao were much photographed toasting one another — the alliance was as fragile as its predecessors.

When the decade that brought peace also brought an end to the long and bitter civil war, there were those who recalled the prophetic words of Sir Robert Hart who died as the empire he had served was replaced by a republic. Hart speculated that the Boxer Rebellion had stirred much more than anti-missionary sentiment.

"In fifty years time," Hart suggested, "there will be millions of Boxers in serried ranks... armed, drilled, disciplined, and animated by patriotic — if mistaken — motives. They will make residence in China impossible for foreigners and will take back from foreigners everything foreigners had taken from China."

When the People's Republic of China was born on a sea of red silk flags in Peking's Tiananmen Square on 1st October 1949, it was clear that, as Napoleon had predicted, the Dragon was very much awake. As the nation's new leader put it: "The Chinese people have stood up."

The birth of the new republic had cost much more in terms of human life than had the earlier revolution that launched China into the 20th century. And in the decades to come, more blood would be shed — even in the square billowing with red silk.

In China, red is the colour of joy. When it flooded Tiananmen Square in 1949, it was a symbol of the high hopes that buoyed the thousands who thronged the massive arena.

That potent energy and optimism — so evident to the cameras of the Western press soon to be banished — would carry China through a self-imposed isolation as complete as any initiated by the Sons of Heaven in the Middle Kingdom. Through years of social upheaval as long and dark as those unleashed by the Taiping rebels. And, in the final decades of the 20th century, into a whole new era of encounter.

"Let China sleep for when she awakes she will astonish the world."

Napoleon I

"Our country will never again be an insulted nation. The Chinese people have stood up."

Mao Tse-tung, 1st October 1949

The Treaty Ports

FRINGE ON THE ANCIENT GARMENT

British consular garden party in Amoy, 1907.

THE TREATY PORTS THAT LACED THE COAST OF CHINA IN THE 19TH CENTURY were, in essence, places of encounter: where the land met the sea; where rivers, flowing from the very heart of the empire, joined the ocean; where merchandise was traded; where East met West.

The people living in the ancient walled villages of these coastal cities had always lived by trade — for the rivers on which most were sited carried merchandise from the interior, and merchants carried it further, across the South China Sea, in their trading junks.

An island shrine on the Yangtze River.

When imperial decrees restricted coastal trade, the city ports languished. When they became treaty ports, an extra dimension was added to their trading encounters — and many of them flourished.

To the treaty ports came teas and silks from the interior — plus reports of rebellions, plagues and attacks by coastal pirates. To them came merchants, missionaries and consuls, foreign fleets and the soldiers of fortune who invariably washed up on the China coast in the 19th century.

Above: **Visitors relax at Foochow's Kushan Monastery in 1909.**
Opposite page: **German consular group at Tsingtao, 1905.**

These early foreign footholds in China gave foreigners their first taste of life in the Middle Kingdom and offered China its first windows on the West.

When the treaty ports first opened, China was terra incognita and the ports became welcomed enclaves that isolated early arrivals from the turmoil of Chinese life. Within their boundaries were

well-patrolled, tree-lined streets, familiar church spires and domed and colonnaded buildings that stirred the civic pride of residents. Some clung to the comfort and security of the treaty ports, even when travel restrictions were lifted. Others used them as stepping stones to the empire that lay beyond.

Some of the ports — like Shanghai — were destined to become commercial, financial and industrial centres known throughout the world. Others, like the British naval base at Weihaiwei, would remain sleepy backwaters with barely enough residents to hold a respectable Government House reception.

Main thoroughfare of Mukden, Manchuria.

Almost every port boasted a racecourse that was established as soon as a sizable community existed. Initially small China ponies, used to carrying heavy loads across the Gobi Desert, were raced. These stocky ponies won the devotion of foreign trainers — who claimed they had "fire in their hearts" — and every coastal city had its favourite pony.

When White Russian refugees fled to China, treaty port races were enlivened by superb Russian horsemen — "born in

*Above: **Houseboat excursion near Hangchow.** Opposite page: **The Foochow races, 1907,** featured sturdy China ponies used to heavy loads — including German military gentlemen.*

the saddle" Cossacks or graduates of the Russian Imperial War Academy of St Petersburg — who were much in demand as trainers. At that time interbreeding began between the tall Russian horses and the thick-set China ponies, and the appearance of their offspring, who ran off with all the prizes, created havoc at racecourses.

Extraterritoriality meant that the enclaves of the treaty ports became, effectively, slices of

The Tsingtao Club, the hub of social activities.

British, French or German "soil" set on the coast of China — and each had its own distinctive character.

Tientsin, upriver from the Taku forts — plagued by dust storms, snowstorms or the flooding of the Yellow River — boasted several foreign concessions during its heyday. Its landmarks included a feudal castle built by a Prussian; a miniature railway built by the French; several impressive brass bands established by the British; and a Russian light opera company. When the Yellow River flooded — and pianos and furniture floated on the waters that invaded their homes — the well-sited Tientsin Club became a familiar retreat for all foreigners.

Tsingtao — originally leased by the Germans in 1898 — had the prosperous look of a town in Germany. It boasted an impressive club, well laid-out wide streets lined by buildings and banks and bakeries full of tantalizing aromas. During World War I the Japanese captured it, adding a large fish market, plus cotton and silk mills that Chinese patriots later blew up during the long war of the 1930s.

As Russian influence extended with the opening of the Trans-Siberian railway line in 1898, the onion domes of Russian churches multiplied through Manchuria. The tone of society in Russian concessions sometimes reflected

Above: **Tsingtao, looking like a prosperous German town, welcomed the Prince of Prussia in 1904.**
Opposite page: **Treaty port wedding.**

the extravagance of tsarist Russia. At consular functions, banqueting tables groaned beneath the weight of baked sturgeons, boars' heads, whole deer complete with antlers, and pheasants in full plumage which, when lifted off, revealed succulent, carved meat.

Some coastal cities changed hands numerous times as territorial power games were played out on Chinese

Above: **Weddings, families and social gatherings, Soochow and Tsingtao.** *Opposite page:* **Manchurian port.**

territory. Dairen, on the strategically important Liaotung Peninsula, was captured by the Japanese in 1894, then restored to China, only to be later leased by the Russians. This coveted ice-free port again fell to Japan during the Russo-Japanese War of 1905 and remained in Japanese hands until the end of World War II. At that time Chiang Kai-shek and Stalin signed an agreement making Dairen a free port — and enabling Soviet authorities (still enjoying special rights in Manchuria) to frustrate the movements of Nationalist troops in the province. When Chiang's troops tried to land at Dairen, the Russians refused entry on the

Swatow with various "foreign" representatives.

grounds that it was a commercial port, thus winning valuable time for Communist troops targetting the cities being surrendered by Japan.

In the 19th century, treaty port society was dominated by bachelors. However, when the tedious journey to the Far East was shortened by steamships and the opening of the Suez, the civilizing influence of women ended an era that had been decidedly appealing to some. Household servants quickly learnt to cope with the demands of a sometimes contrary "missy", and fashions in vogue in Europe began to appear at racecourses and theatres soon to be cleverly copied — by Chinese tailors.

With a transient foreign population, arrivals and departures were very much a part of treaty port life. The Peninsula and Oriental Line (P & O) liners — dubbed the "fishing fleet" — carried young women from Britain eager to find themselves husbands. And if P & O didn't provide a treaty port man with a suitable partner, there was always "home" leave and the chance that a well selected fiancé would follow him out East. However, shipboard romances flowered during tropic nights at sea, and not a few young men waited in vain for ladies who made other liaisons on the P & O voyage out.

By the turn of the century the journey to China was further shortened by the debut of a train de luxe — the Trans-Siberian International Express. This first land link between Western Europe and the Far East made it possible for treaty port residents on leave in London to journey across Europe, Russia and China by rail and steamer. The first Englishman to undertake the journey in 1902 was convinced that the Russians were merely using the railway to expand their presence in Manchuria.

Chinese women seldom ventured beyond their homes in the 19th century.

"The railway in its entirety is flimsy and liable to collapse almost everywhere," he wrote waspishly. However, others relished this "ambulant palace of luxury" where one dined on roast partridge and red wine from the Imperial Crimean estates in company that might include a Russian or Tatar princess, a Cossack general or a famous French explorer.

But then came World War I, which marked the beginning of the end for the treaty ports. In the 1920s, several foreign powers relinquished their concessions and in 1943 Britain and America took the lead in voluntarily abolishing all "unequal treaties" wrung from China. With concessions abolished, China reclaimed itself with pride.

The treaty ports were once likened to "a fringe stitched along the hem of an ancient garment". Now China severed the alien threads, and rejected the social and political gospels that the treaty ports had enshrined.

Most foreign residents hurriedly bought one-way tickets on ships that, in less troubled times, were decked with streamers and bunting to welcome new arrivals.

Inevitably some were reluctant to leave Chinese coastal cities that had been home to several generations of their families. For a while they lingered on — in offices overlooking the bund; in homes where both blackwood furniture and chinz had found a place; in treaty ports now more familiar than a distant homeland.

Japan was well aware that China had long referred to it contemptuously as a nation of "dwarf barbarians".

Dinner in Manchuria to celebrate the birthday of the Japanese Emperor.

PEKING

SEAT OF THE THRONE

Vendors turned Peking's thoroughfares into markets.

Opposite page: **Peking was the final destination for camel trains that crossed the Gobi Desert.**

Tranquil hillside monasteries always had a cup of welcoming tea for the pilgrim or passing traveller.

PEKING PROVIDED AN APPROPRIATELY THEATRICAL BACKDROP FOR SOME OF THE most dramatic diplomatic and military encounters between China and the West.

It witnessed the first encounter between a British envoy and a Chinese Emperor in 1793; the first major defeat of the Chinese empire; the heady "Hundred Days" of a Western-inspired reform movement; and, finally, the Boxer turmoil that closed the 19th century.

From 1860, when the Convention of Peking permitted foreign residence in the capital, an additional enclave for diplomats was added to the already well-defined quarters of the capital. Each quarter — the Chinese City on the outer limits; the Tatar City that accommodated the legations; the Imperial City that embraced the Forbidden City — was girdled by high walls.

To the falcons wheeling above the plain from which the city rose, it must have looked like a complex puzzle — walls within walls, moats within moats. And beyond it, some one hundred miles north, lay further fortifications — the Great Wall.

From Prospect Hill, the city revealed aspects not visible from its dusty, unsanitary streets: the brilliant enamel of temple roofs; the graceful curves of upturned eaves; the sheen of artificial lakes; and hidden gardens bright with flowering shrubs.

The empire's capital had once been located further south, at Sian (where the Empress Dowager retreated after the Boxer catastrophe), but it was thought prudent to relocate closer

Chinese dignitaries at the Ming Tombs that lay to the nor■

to the troublesome northern frontier and the Great Wall that linked the nation's northern defences.

Thus the capital was plagued by the winds that blew off the Gobi Desert, stirring great storms and leaving mounds of sand heaped against the city walls. In summer, hot winds fanned the city. In winter, the savage cold littered its streets with frozen corpses that were routinely collected by municipal carts at dawn.

To early foreign visitors Peking presented unforgettable images of amazing splendour and appalling squalor. John Thomson, one of the first photographers to record the fascination of street life in China, recounted the horror of frozen bodies heaped at the city gates; and pleasure at the prosperous merchants in silks, who presided over jade and lacquerware. The façades of their shops, he noted, were so elaborately carved, painted and gilded "they looked as if they ought to be under glass cases."

Peking.

Thomson's camera was viewed as a "dark, mysterious instrument" by the often hostile audience that gathered to watch him at work. However, its ability to fix an image soon encouraged people to bring ageing parents for portraits that became part of the Confucian ritual of honouring ancestors.

During his 1872 visit, Thomson's camera captured the extraordinary everyday images that flowed through the streets of Peking: the mandarin with his retinue wielding bamboo rods to clear a path; Chinese women mincing and swaying on bound feet; itinerant chefs engulfed in the steam of their mobile kitchens; craftsmen mending blue-and-white porcelain with tiny brass rivets; "honey carts" loaded with barrels of night soil destined for nearby fields; herbalists prescribing potions for rheumatic old men with "wind in the bones"; letter writers and calligraphists whose sure brush strokes conveyed news and the characters of a couplet; coolies with laden bamboo shoulder poles; silk-curtained sedan chairs and bone-shaking carts; streetside barbers and ear cleaners, dentists and pedlars — and teahouse patrons, sucking on long-stemmed pipes, enjoying the spectacle of the passing parade.

No street was complete without its showmen — its peepshow operators and jugglers, ballad singers and fortune-tellers. Peking opera performers in gaudy satin lured audiences to mat-shed theatres, and even old clothes men vied for attention at streetside auctions. The latter drew appreciative audiences by investing each garment with an appealing history. Pulling out a fur coat, the auctioneer might evoke the memory of the family it came from: "This fur was worn by the head of the illustrious Chang family, during the year of the great frost when the cold was so intense words froze and hung from men's lips. Thousands died, but as for Chang — all honour to his memory — he put on this coat and it brought summer to his blood. How much say you for it?"

When foreigners first encountered the capital, camel drivers and muleteers carried much of the merchandise transported to and from the city. A British merchant sending tea chests to Russia on the backs of camels found his customers delighted with the flavour of their brews, but when the Trans-Siberian railway replaced camels, they reported a disappointing decline in flavour. Research

Peking falconers with their hooded birds of prey.

revealed that perspiration from the camel's back, absorbed by the chests during the overland journey, had added a subtle flavour that later consignments — even when packed with camel hair — failed to restore.

Foreign diplomats permitted residence in the capital from 1860 tended to isolate themselves in the legation quarter bounded on three sides by the walls of the Tatar City, the gates of which were barred each night at sundown.

When Dr George Morrison, correspondent for The Times of London, acquired a house in the Chinese quarter of the capital foreign eyebrows were raised. "I live in a Chinese house... alone with my books

on China, cut off by dirt streets from the rest of the foreign community,"
he wrote with obvious satisfaction.

But he could not avoid the less-than-adventurous fare

provided at legation banquets. At a
dinner to mark Queen Victoria's
Diamond Jubilee, guests waded
through a banquet not unlike
that being served in dozens of
far-flung outposts where — as in
Peking — the mid-year temperatures
were torrid: Jubilee Soup, Oyster
Patties, Roast Beef, Boiled Ham, Tongue
in Jelly, Roast Lamb, Spring Chicken and
Plum Pudding.

China's elder statesman,
Viceroy Li Hung-chang.

Foreign diplomats in Peking hardly ventured into the Chinese city
unless they wished to indulge in its vices. Well-appointed opium divans were
an exotic lure to be sampled at least once, while singsong houses offering
"lily-footed" ladies were patronized by all — from the Emperor to fresh-faced
consular recruits.

Emperor Hsien-feng, whose early death was due in no small part to
dissipation, preferred the bawdy houses, pornographic peepshows and transvestite performances of Peking's
outer city. However, his mandarins were admonished to refrain from summoning singsong girls to their
banquets. This imperative resulted in the extraordinary rise in popularity of young apprentices being trained
for female roles with Peking opera troupes. By the mid-19th century these ambivalent youth had become
the darlings of Peking society. Encased in silks, their faces whitened and rouged, they indulged their
mandarin patrons in a coy game with a wine glass passed, mouth to mouth — knowing that the mandarin's
wife preferred him to keep company with a effeminate boy than a singsong girl who aspired to a concubine.

Near the gate of the Imperial City was another curiosity — a hereditary family business that specialized in castration. The only men allowed in the Forbidden City were castrati, and poverty ensured that there was no shortage of candidates for employment within the imperial household. The eunuch's severed parts, known as "the precious", were kept in sealed jars to be produced during annual inspections by the palace's Chief Eunuch. The last Emperor, P'u Yi, finally broke the centuries-long tradition when he dismissed the last palace eunuchs in 1923.

The Emperor, who lost his imperial title a year later, made other breaks with the past. He installed a cinema in the Palace of Happiness where Fatty Arbuckle films were shown and later added a lawn tennis court to the Forbidden City. When the sixteen-year-old acquired two consorts, the three newly-weds were reported sailing through the royal apartments on bicycles.

However, the light-hearted fun of early marriage did not last. One of P'u Yi's consorts abandoned him, the other quickly became addicted to the drug that still debilitated the nation.

A concerted international effort had been made to suppress opium in the first decade of the 20th century, and in 1909 an International Opium Conference in Shanghai reached agreement on abolishing the trade. However, predictably, illicit

Peking's craftsmen plied their trades in the city's busy markets.

drugs merely went underground, and twenty years after the last divans supposedly closed their doors — in 1917 — there were estimated to be twenty-two million addicts in China.

In Peking, twenty-two thousand ounces of opium were burnt to mark "National Anti-Opium Day" in 1937. But while the government suppressed the drug, illegal networks both manufactured and pushed them — particularly in Japanese concessions where opium pipes and lamps were openly sold, and scores of narcotic plants existed.

For Chinese peasants living in north-eastern provinces, the acres of white poppies they harvested provided a meagre living. For the numberless poor who roamed Peking's streets, opium "sweet dreams" were seductive.

In Peking they had a special term for the homeless and starving: "the people of bitterness".

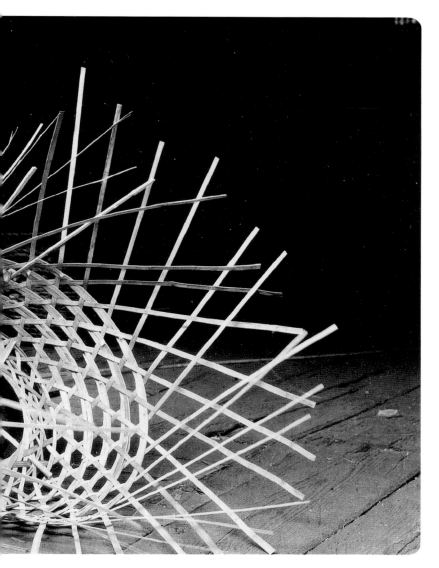

They caused municipal authorities no end of irritation when city streets needed to look their best for public functions.

When she visited Peking in 1913, writer and traveller Violet Markham noted the still pervasive corruption and the wretched conditions in which most people lived.

Later she wrote prophetically: "Little wonder that Communism has captured China. Every condition exists of poverty, want and distress, conducive to that evil growth. But the Chinaman remains a sturdy and passionate individualist, and whatever home-grown variety of Communism he may adopt, he will, I think, be difficult to regiment from Moscow or any distant centre."

Markham visited when Yuan Shih-k'ai held the reins of power and was reluctant to meet republican wishes to relocate the capital in Nanking, away from his military power base in Peking. However, when Chiang Kai-shek united China under a Nationalist Government in 1929, Nanking became the capital, as Dr Sun Yat-sen, Father of the Republic, had wished.

Peking, the capital during five dynasties was suddenly no longer the hub of power. Renamed Peiping — Northern Peace — it had to wait two decades until restored to centre stage, with the birth of the People's Republic of China in Tiananmen Squarein 1949.

Opposite page: **Northern defences were linked into a "Great Wall", the empire's most famous landmark.**

Shanghai

CITY BY THE SEA

Above: **British family in Shanghai, 1914.**
Opposite page: **The band stand in the Shanghai's Public Gardens; the English Club.**

*Above: **Wheel barrows carried goods and people across the city.***
*Opposite page: **Elaborately-dressed hair was favoured by Chinese ladies in their silks.***

WHEN, IN THE 1840S, IT WAS ONE OF THE FIRST FIVE TREATY PORTS OPENED TO foreign trade in the wake of the Opium War, Shanghai was a walled city of three hundred thousand on the mud flats where the Whangpoo River and Soochow Creek met, several miles from the Yangtze estuary.

When relinquishing a stretch of waterfront to the victorious foreign powers who carved it into concessions — one for British and American residents, the International Settlement, another for the French — Peking no doubt took pleasure in the knowledge that Shanghai was well named. For the "city by the sea" was frequently engulfed by it. Prone to flooding at high tide, its mud flats were deluged by several feet of water when the tide was backed by the force of a typhoon.

The treaty port's location was the key to its prosperity. Its river and creek offered access to the trading ports on the mighty Yangtze River and the Grand Canal. Its harbour, though given to silting, was sheltered. And the Shanghainese had always looked outward — to the ocean that

The domed Hong Kong and Shanghai Banking Corporation on the Bund.

provided the livelihood of fishermen and merchants engaged in the junk trade. Their enterprise would be a vital factor in the transformation of the city over the next century.

The first foreign firms to exploit these assets — and eleven were established within the first year — were quick to construct an embankment, a "bund", along the river bank. In this way the muddy tidal foreshore of the Whangpoo was able to accommodate jetties and the settlement's first

waterfront offices. The treaty port's most famous landmark had been created.

The early foreign frontrunners — who would dominate the Shanghai Municipal Council, the governing body of the International Settlement — included several of the companies once restricted to the factory area of Canton's foreshore.

The British company Jardine, Matheson and Co and the American firm Russell & Co, along with prominent Parsee merchants active in the China trade, began to develop the web of trade and shipping that soon linked the city port to the wider world. And these same companies provided the capital for the region's first bank, The Hong Kong and Shanghai Banking Corporation, whose domed offices on the bund provided the city with another landmark.

In the 19th century, Shanghai quickly claimed the lead among treaty ports, and even eclipsed the precocious colonial entrepôt of Hong Kong.

Fine shops and fancy hotels flanked Nanking and Bubbling Well Roads where rickshaws and overburdened coolies jostled with handcarts, horses and carriages and, later, trams and cars. Banks from across the world established a presence. The first, in 1847, was the Oriental Banking Corporation, followed soon after by the Chartered Mercantile Bank of India, London and China. Soon the city's banks — the First National Bank of New York, the Netherland Trading Society, the Yokohama Specie Bank, the Russo-Chinese Bank, the Banque de l'Indochine and the Imperial Bank of China — reflected its cosmopolitan character.

The zigzag bridge deflected evil spirits from the Willow Teahouse, a famous city landmark.

By the 1930s, Shanghai was Asia's busiest international port and had joined the ranks — along with London, Paris, New York and Tokyo — of the world's most cosmopolitan cities. Its foreign population ran to one hundred thousand and represented forty-six different countries.

With almost every international company doing business in China basing its headquarters in Shanghai, it became the commercial hub of the nation; the place where decisions were made, and deals were done.

And Chinese entrepreneurs were quick to exploit its trading opportunities and to invest in foreign enterprises — for treaty port extraterritoriality enabled them to bypass Chinese bureaucratic interference. When Russell & Co established the Shanghai Steam Navigation Company in 1861, Chinese merchants provided the bulk of the capital. And when the opening of the Suez Canal in 1869 boosted shipping even further, Chinese merchants formed the China Merchants' Navigation Company — under the aegis of the

powerful Viceroy Li Hung-chang — and acquired a substantial share of the tonnage moving through Shanghai's busy harbour.

Initially those who lived in the International Settlement claimed that all the city's major decisions were in the hands of a few British taipans who conducted business from No. 3 The Bund — the Shanghai Club — or from the grandstand at the Shanghai Race Club where China ponies helped to increase the fortunes of their owners.

But in the early decades of the 20th century, the Japanese commercial, military and naval presence far outstripped that of the British. By the late 1930s, Japanese-owned mills dominated the industrial area and there were twice as many Japanese as British living in Shanghai — in a concession predictably dubbed "Little Tokyo".

For its well-heeled residents, Shanghai offered a host of daily diversions from mahjong and tiffin parties to country rides at Jessfield Park on the outskirts of the International Settlement. The traditions of Britain were faithfully nurtured: croquet and cricket was played on manicured greens; hunting horns resounded through the hills beyond the city; and shooting parties returned triumphant with partridges and pheasants, and antlers worthy of any mantelpiece.

At the city's smart hotels, like the Cathay Hotel where Noël Coward wrote his brittle comedy, Private Lives, the fashionable set met for tea dances that lasted until midnight — just about the time the glitzy neon city came alive.

But the city port's sophistication existed alongside the shadow of a more sinister Shanghai. Born of the Opium War, it never quite shrugged off the vices that kept company with the illicit trade. Its alleys had their share of opium dens and brothels and, the 1920s and '30s, its underworld rivalled Chicago's. Gangland bosses even rose to positions of prominence — in the French Concession's police force, on the Shanghai Municipal Council, and occasionally on the boards of local charities.

In Shanghai anything and everything was for sale. Racketeers sold protection to the city's workforce — and even pickpockets and beggars paid to work the streets and parade their deformities.

Parents sold their daughters and husbands sold unwanted concubines to the singsong houses of a city that boasted more prostitutes than any other. Children sold their labour — for a few cents an hour — to textile mills and match factories. And blonde White Russian aristocrats, who didn't even own the shimmering, skin-tight dresses they wore, sold their company on the dance floors of the city's countless dance halls.

In the 1920s Shanghai's fabulous wealth nudged the meanest of poverty. Exploitation was rife and the city's massive labour force provided febrile ground for Communist activists — indeed the Chinese Communist Party was born at a meeting in the French Concession. Later in that decade, its streets ran with blood when Generalissimo Chiang Kai-shek ordered his Nationalist troops to purge the city of his political rivals.

Like most treaty ports, Shanghai inevitably became a sanctuary for refugees. Each wave of turmoil — the Taiping rebellion, the Sino-Japanese War — emptied thousands of refugees into its overcrowded streets.

The unceasing flow of life in Shanghai's busy streets.

In the 20th century, it also became a sanctuary for refugees from neighbouring countries and from Europe. In 1917, after the Bolshevik Revolution, some fifteen thousand White Russians sought refuge in the city. In the 1930s, Jews fleeing Nazi Germany swelled the ranks of the city's refugees. Many arrived

Foreigners return to the city-port after a successful wildfowl shooting trip.

Streetside barbers were as much a feature of the city-port as its teahouses.

IN THE 17TH CENTURY, AS FOREIGN MERCHANTS BEGAN TO GATHER ON THE OUTER edges of the Chinese empire, the Ch'ing court decided to open a single port to foreign trade. It selected Canton, capital of its most southerly maritime province, and a city that already evinced a curious desire to trade with the outside world.

Arab traders had found their way to the city port on the Pearl River estuary during the 10th century, and six centuries later they were followed by the Portuguese, the Dutch and, later, their British rivals. The latter established the largest and best-appointed factory on the waterfront to which the merchants were restricted.

Canton offered 19th-century merchants their first glimpse behind "the veil" that British Secretary of State for War, Thomas Babington Macaulay, claimed shrouded the Chinese empire in mystery. The city port's heavily fortified river was also the site of the first skirmishes between British gunboats and Chinese war junks. And Lintin Island, in the Pearl River estuary, became the first base for the opium smuggling that sparked the Anglo-Chinese war.

Part of Canton's foreign enclave — the orderly, tree-lined island of Shameen.

When Canton was one of the first five treaty ports to open in 1842, its viceroy and gentry continued to refuse residence in the city to foreigners. Their arrogance enraged the governor of neighbouring Hong Kong, Sir John Bowring, who claimed that unless Canton, the "gate to China", was subdued, the situation of foreigners — still penned within waterfront factories — would remain untenable.

Subdued the city certainly was in the subsequent war that involved both British and French troops. Finally the right to residence in the walled city was secured. However, the first close encounters with Canton convinced foreign merchants to rapidly replace their destroyed factories with a concession that kept the congested city at arms length.

Though Canton's Silk Street and Jade Alley, its pagodas and temples, intrigued foreigners, the city's execution ground and the criminals that were publicly paraded on its streets made them uneasy of a system of justice that was both brutal and arbitrary. They were grateful that the Treaty of Bogue, signed a year after the treaty ports were opened, secured them extraterritorial rights.

The need for extraterritoriality — the right of foreigners to live under their own laws rather than those of China — had been illustrated by the notorious Lady Hughes affair of 1784 when an English sailor, firing a salute from a British vessel in Canton, had accidentally killed a Chinese boatman. Much to the disgust of the merchants, the British East India Company had met Chinese demands to hand over the unfortunate sailor. He was subsequently tried by a Chinese court, convicted and strangled. The Company was accused of purchasing commercial interests "with the blood of the gunner of the Lady Hughes" — the last Englishman abandoned to Chinese justice.

While Europe's medieval castles had boasted their own instruments of torture — ranging from bone-breaking wheels to a spiked iron frame that locked its victims in a deadly embrace — the sheer range of punishments and tortures still practised in China alarmed foreigners. The Ch'ing code comprised of "Five Punishments": beatings (both light and heavy) with bamboo canes, penal servitude, exile and death. The latter ranged from strangulation and decapitation to the lingering "death by a thousand cuts" for a range of crimes (including treason and patricide) categorized as the "Ten Abominations".

Collective responsibility — which made a Governor-General culpable for the residents within his jurisdiction, and the Hong merchants responsible for the behaviour of foreign traders in Canton — meant

that in cases of serious crimes, such as treason, the male relatives of the convicted were also beheaded.

Crime and punishment was a very public spectacle in imperial China. Severed heads in baskets were displayed on city walls and every city had its execution ground. Judging by the number of photographs of well-attired gentlemen posed beside headless bodies, the harshness of the Chinese criminal code held a certain gruesome fascination for foreigners. In 1851, the British consul in Canton witnessed the rapid dispatch of thirty-three men, each with a single blow of the executioner's sword — in three minutes.

Executioners were open to bribes to end the misery of their victims with

Imperial China made visible use of an array of punishments — from the wearing of can

a single, skilful stroke, just as court officials could be induced to lighten the strokes of the canes they wielded.

Foreign residents encountering wretched petty criminals wearing heavy wooden collars — cangues

— that required relatives to share their public humiliation when feeding them, were understandably relieved to be free of a judicial system so different from their own.

Once the foreign community in Canton was established on its concession — the reclaimed sandbank of Shameen, on the Canton River — it felt more secure. Shameen was separated from the sometimes alarming city

xecution.

in which they had chosen to live and work by a narrow creek. And in times of turmoil, the two bridges linking it with the mainland were guarded by soldiers dispatched from nearby Hong Kong.

Handsome houses and offices soon emerged from the luxuriant tapestry of greenery that quickly transformed the mud flat. Merchants who chose to live in Shameen — operating mainly as agents for shipping and banking concerns with headquarters elsewhere — were well aware that their Hong Kong counterparts considered Canton a trading backwater. But Shameen was a comfortable place to live, offering desirable amenities such as public gardens, bowling greens and croquet lawns, plus the diversions of annual regattas and horse races.

From the 1860s, the Hong Kong, Canton and Macao Steamship Company made twice daily sailings, bringing returning residents and Hong Kong visitors in need of "a change of air" and pace. They found local markets well supplied with fruit, vegetables and poultry, and in winter partridge, quail and wildfowl.

Above: **Dr Sun Yat-sen plotted revolution from his Canton base, supported by the city's military forces.**
Oppositive page: **The last known photograph of Dr Sun Yat-sen, architect of the republic, who died in 1925.**

Snipe shooting became a popular weekend sport for Shameen's residents and, from November to March, duck, goose and teal attracted hunters to the wetlands around the riverside forts. But the bird that most appealed to Western palates was the diminutive ricebird that arrived in vast flocks to feast on the ripening paddy fields in autumn — and was caught by farmers dragging the fields with nets at night. "These delicious little birds, scarcely as large as a canary, are celebrated for their succulence and flavour," enthused a 19th-century visitor. "When fried in breadcrumbs by a Cantonese cook, they are the most luxurious eating."

Free from the traffic that later jammed the streets of Canton and neighbouring Hong Kong, Shameen retained its tranquility, even during the first decade of the 20th century, when the city became the base for Dr Sun Yat-sen's republican dreams.

Sun, the Father of the Republic, was born near Canton. Following a long-established tradition in an area with poor soil and little prospects, Sun's brother sought a livelihood overseas. When he had established a prosperous business in Hawaii, he sent for Sun and his mother.

Early years of hardship in a peasant family helped to shape Sun's political philosophies and to win him the support of fellow revolutionaries. When he returned to Canton after medical studies in Hong Kong,

Above: **Crowds greet Dr Sun's funeral cortege when it finally reached Canton.**
Opposite page: **The city-port of Canton was the southern gateway to Imperial China.**

he freely donated his services to the needy to gather a following. Canton became the focus for his first attempt at revolution and although the 1895 uprising failed to secure the city as a revolutionary base, it created the first martyrs of the revolution.

During the revolution, the merchants and missionaries of Shameen watched events unfold from the security of their foreign enclave. At that time, the three hundred residents depended for their defence on the forty-four men of the Shameen Defence Corps. However, as a precaution the British army in Hong Kong dispatched members of the Baluchistan Infantry who were billeted in Shameen for more than a year.

When in the 1920s the fragile alliance between Nationalists and Communists erupted, the residents of Shameen were once again grateful to be removed from the scenes of carnage that followed a three-day Communist coup in Canton. During this reign of terror, thousands of lives were lost and homes gutted. When Nationalist troops reclaimed the city the bloodbath was repeated, for it was easy to identify local Communists by the telltale neck stains of red scarves worn during the coup. More than five thousand local Communists were executed.

Though Canton's political profile developed in the early decades of the 20th century, it was eclipsed as a city port that lived by foreign trade. Its harbour was shallow and given to silting. It could not compete with its colonial neighbour, Hong Kong, or with the infrastructure for trade and investment available in treaty ports such as Shanghai.

While it retained an interest in the tea trade it had monopolized through the 18th and much of the 19th century, when exports declined with the flowering of tea gardens in India and Ceylon ironically established with indentured Chinese labour, the city port lost its former status — as the "gate to China", the first foreign foothold.

Weihaiwei

A Summer Place

TO MANY FOREIGNERS WHO LIVED IN NORTHERN CHINA IN THE 20TH CENTURY'S EARLY decades, Weihaiwei was a summer place — a small and pretty treaty port that was as tranquil as Shanghai was boisterous.

In July and August this British concession, acquired at the turn of the century, enjoyed a lively social life. Visitors from Peking, Shanghai and Hong Kong savoured its uncongested coastline, picnicked at Half Moon Bay, attended regattas, gymkhanas and amateur theatricals, and made good use of the naval base's sporting facilities.

Government House receptions, that at other times were woefully small, had the added dash of a naval presence, for the summer base boasted as many as a dozen ships of war.

Come winter, however, the visitors left, the navy shrank to a token presence of a single vessel, and the officers who presided over the civil administration of the concession were marooned in the misery of a bitter winter.

British and Chinese officials enjoyed harmonious relations in Weihaiwei.

Set on the strategically important Liaotung Peninsula, Weihaiwei had been developed as a naval base as part of China's "self-strengthening". However, during the Sino-Japanese War of 1894 the base suffered the ignominy of being captured from the rear by Japanese soldiers who turned its guns on the Chinese boats in the harbour.

The Colonial Office was less than enthusiastic at the acquisition of the four hundred square miles of territory in German-dominated Shantung. It was leased by the British, along with Hong Kong's New Territories, at a time when China was being systematically carved into "spheres of influence" by the imperial powers.

During the unseemly scramble for territory and concessions in the late 1890s, Britain was determined not to lose its status, and its territorial share of China. When it was known that Germany coveted Weihaiwei, that was reason enough to lease it, thus frustrating a rival — while keeping an eye on its expanding influence.

James Stewart Lockhart, Commissioner of Weihaiwei.

Set in a remote corner of Shantung Province, Weihaiwei's somewhat sere coastline reminded its first Commissioner of his native Scotland — especially when wrapped in the bitter chill of winter.

James Stewart Lockhart's appointment as Weihaiwei's Commissioner in 1902 took him from the fast-paced commercial and social world of Hong Kong (where he had been Colonial Secretary) to a sleepy outpost that, as one observer noted, had "absolutely no commercial resources."

However, Lockhart and his assistant, a fellow Scot and China scholar, Reginald Johnston — who was later appointed tutor to the Manchu dynasty's last Emperor, P'u Yi — were determined to make Weihaiwei a concession of consequence. But while their fluency in the language and love of things Chinese endeared them to the local population and the viceroy of the province, they faced an uphill battle.

Despite the fact that Weihaiwei was a free port, it had neither roads nor rail (the Germans owned both railway and mining concessions) to transport goods from the interior. Eventually Lockhart realistically shelved his dreams and concentrated on projects that were achievable — like reafforestation. Planting literally thousands of acacias, firs and willows, he turned the roadsides of Weihaiwei into areas of lush greenery.

One of the duties of his administration was the collection of land taxes within the concession which Chinese farmers willingly paid, as they were lower than those previously levied by the Emperor. Another was administering a system of justice, which also met with local approval.

Johnston presided over the magistrate's courts combining the "duties of Registrar-General

(Protector of Chinese), Puisne Judge, Police Magistrate and Captain-Superintendent of Police". Although the local jail held few prisoners and serious crime was rare, the magistrate heard both civil and criminal cases, and his frustration at his case load was sometimes evident. In one letter he described a case in which the principal witness, a poor coolie, lied so consistently that he lost the sympathy of the court. When he ultimately revealed the truth, he was given a month's imprisonment for contempt of court. "Asked why he had annoyed everyone by telling so many lies," Johnston recorded, "the coolie replied, 'The truth is very valuable, you can only use it once'."

The Commissioner visiting the Governor of Shantung in 1903.

In Weihaiwei, time seemed to have stood still and traditions and beliefs long jettisoned in republican China still lingered in the territory's three hundred villages. By the time the territory was handed back to China its only significant export had been that of some one hundred and fifty thousand Chinese labourers, sent to the European front during World War I.

Like all treaty ports, Weihaiwei offered visitors and its administrators an often graphic glimpse of Chinese life. For most of the period that the territory was under British rule harvests were good, but in 1919 crops failed throughout north China, leaving an estimated one hundred thousand people in the territory with empty rice bowls.

Lockhart organized relief, but the peasants, weakened by famine, later fell prey to an epidemic of cholera that took the lives of over five thousand. Johnstone himself contracted the disease and was confined to a sanitorium.

The very basic improvements to the unsanitary conditions in which most people lived, which were long overdue, were subsequently initiated by Lockhart.

After twenty years in what had sometimes seemed to him as a sentence imposed by his enemies in the Colonial Office, Lockhart left Weihaiwei. He had maintained a peaceful corner of the Chinese empire, and later republic, through two of the most tumultuous decades that China would know.

Reginald Johnston with a portrait of King Edward VII prior to its presentation to a Chinese duke in 1904.

In 1927, Lockhart's former assistant, Reginald Johnston, returned to the territory as Weihaiwei's last Commissioner, having completed his secondment by the Colonial Office as tutor to Emperor P'u Yi. While in the Forbidden City — which horrified him with its "follies and futilities" — he had abolished the imperial yellow sedan chair that carried the young Emperor to lessons and had taught him, among other things, to play lawn tennis and ride a bicycle. His secondment ended when Emperor P'u Yi left Peking to live in a house in the British concession at Tientsin.

After his years in Peking Johnston was pleased to return to this quiet corner of China, and to wind down the administration for return to its rightful owners.

During his two decades in office, Lockhart had an abrasive relationship with the Colonial Office which had consistently refused requests for additional funding. However, when he left Weihaiwei, it conceded that the territory had been run "with such a combination of deference to Chinese custom, with British justice and incorruptibility, that the inhabitants have come to regard the British occupation as a sort of golden age."

In April 1930, Weihaiwei — never much more than "a summer place" during the brief time it served as a treaty port — was finally returned to China.

Within a few years, Lockhart's most abiding monument — the now mature stands of acacias, firs and roadside willows that painted the sere countryside with swathes of green — had proved irresistible as kindling to villagers of a district acknowledged to be one of the poorest in China.

The Catholic Mission School at Weihaiwei.

Hong Kong and Macao

THE COLONIAL CITIES

Ferries and sampans, naval vessels and merchant ships crowded Hong Kong's "safe and commodious" harbour.

Above: **Dr Sun Yat-sen, "Father of the Republic"** *(seated) with* **Sir Claude Severn, Colonial Secretary,**
at Government House in 1911. Standing *(far left) is* **Dr Kai Ho Kai.**
Both Captain Henry May, head of the Hong Kong Police and Sir Cecil Clementi, *(right) became future governors of Hong Kong.*
Opposite page: **Sir Frederick Lugard with members of the Legislative Council**
on the steps of Government House with Commissioner of Foreign Affairs Li Cheng Feng and his party.

WHEN FOREIGN MERCHANTS FIRST BEGAN TO TRADE IN TEAS AND SILKS IN CHINA, they spent the winter trading seasons in Canton and summers in Macao.

The Portuguese settlement — set on a spit of land two miles long and barely half a mile wide — was conveniently located sixty-five miles south of Canton. China tolerated the small settlement, established in the 16th century, as a reward for Portuguese help in dispatching a tiresome band of pirates that had plagued its coastal cities.

To foreign merchants frustrated by Canton's restrictions, even this slender limb of land — eventually enlarged beyond recognition through reclamation — became a welcomed respite. In handsome summer homes, the taipans of the China Trade entertained lavishly; and behind the pillared porticoes of their Macao headquarters they plotted endlessly — not only trading strategies for the coming season, but political strategies for opening China to unrestricted trade.

The aggressive breed of merchant who summered in Macao in the 18th and early 19th centuries were generally contemptuous of their lethargic Portuguese hosts. It surprised them to learn that in the 17th century Macao had successfully repelled an attack by the predatory Dutch,

The waterfront of the Portuguese settlement.

in a well-armed vessel, when the town's forts were incomplete and its able-bodied men were buying silks in Canton. A brave fighting force of Portuguese soldiers and mostly drunken African slaves faced the invaders, engaging in fierce hand-to-hand combat. Luck was with them, and a cannon fired from Monte Fort exploded the powder magazine of the attacking vessel, causing such devastation that the Dutch fled in disarray. The Portuguese attributed their victory to the appearance of St John the Baptist in their ranks at the height of the battle. Thereafter the saint became the town's patron and the "miracle" of its salvation was much celebrated.

British merchants envied the Portuguese their base and were astonished that having secured an early trading advantage — they first sailed up the Pearl River in 1513 — the merchants of Macao now seemed content to languish in elegantly decaying mansions. Portugal had enjoyed a trading monopoly that linked China and Japan with colonial outposts at Goa and Malacca — until the Emperor opened Canton to all foreign traders in 1685.

A century later a British observer recorded "the busy and unceasing industry of the Chinese and the indolence of the Portuguese sauntering about the square of the senate in the intervals between Matins and Vespers." It was not uncommon, he noted, to be accosted by men in threadbare finery, soliciting charity.

Others were charmed by the city of "churches and priests, endless bells and great gardens". Certainly Macao induced an unhurried pace in visitors who explored its boulevards and cobbled streets among red-turban Parsees, Chinese compradors and African slaves attending Portuguese grandees. It offered much to delight the eye of the 19th-century traveller: the sweep of its esplanade — the Praia Grande; the patterned tiles and wrought

Cluttered rooftops crowded the Macao waterfront.

iron of palacios that rivalled those in Portugal; the busts of Portuguese heroes shaded by frangipani and banyan.

To hard-headed traders based in Macao in the 19th century, Macao's two harbours were less than satisfactory for the East Indiamen and clippers of the China trade. And when British merchants began to feel the need to secure a trading base of their own — beyond the menace of the mandarins of Canton — they did not have to look far.

Across the Pearl River estuary from Macao lay the island of Hong Kong. Known mainly to fisherfolk and pirates, it was separated from the mainland by a sheltered, deep-water harbour that had been pronounced "safe and commodious" by the ill-fated Lord Napier. British merchants were convinced that this asset, plus the island's location, would ensure its future as a thriving entrepôt.

When Hong Kong became one of the spoils of the Opium War, merchant princes such as William Jardine and John Dent were quick to relocate and secure the prime waterfront sites that would accommodate warehouses, company messes and private mansions set in spectacular gardens.

The secession of Hong Kong, and the opening of the first five treaty ports as part of the 1842 Treaty of Nanking, were landmark events in the 19th-century encounter of East and West in China.

The secure base enabled the merchants to form banks that would service the rapid development of the colonial island and its treaty port sisters. It also provided a convenient headquarters for the fledgling consular services that took root in each of the coastal outposts and for the British army and navy.

Soon gracefully arcaded Victorian buildings rose along its waterfront and the island was being heralded as one of the glittering prizes of empire. The fact that much of its early development was financed by opium mattered little to those who dubbed the colonial island "a little England in the eastern seas".

Colonial Secretary James Stewart Lockhart and Legislative Councillor Dr Kai Ho-kai at the opening of the Po Leung Kuk in 1896.

Queen's Road — the city's commercial heart.

In fact the frisson of its opium smuggling, combined with the refined comforts of Victorian society, made Hong Kong appealing to an adventurous breed of travellers.

In 1878, Isabella Bird explored the colonial city in a sedan and observed: "A bamboo chair, with two lean coolies, carried me at a swinging pace through streets as steep as those of Genoa. Most are so steep as to be impassable for wheeled vehicles, and some are merely great flights of stairs arched over by dense foliaged trees," she wrote. "It has green balconies with festoons of creepers, lofty houses, people and costumes of all nations, processions of Portuguese priests and nuns. All its many-coloured life is seen to full

advantage under this blue sky and brilliant sun."

While Macao declined behind its pastel shutters and fading façades, its failures served as a spectre that would haunt Hong Kong. From the outset the colonial island exploited every commercial advantage that came its way — from the advent of steam to the arrival of the telegraph. It also sharpened survival skills that were a consequence of its location — both geographical and political.

China had always viewed the growth of the fledgling colony with displeasure and when, soon after it was ceded, the Emperor learned that an early typhoon had destroyed all of its buildings — with the exception of the Jardine Matheson opium warehouse — he repaired to a temple to give grateful thanks to Heaven. However, even as he made ritual sacrifices, the precocious island was rebuilding itself with an energy it exhibited throughout its extraordinary history.

Located on the doorstep of China, Hong Kong soon appreciated that it would suffer the aftershocks of every paroxysm that seized its giant neighbour. Flood, famine and rebellion deposited on its doorstep hungry people seeking the protection of its foreign flag. The Taiping Rebellion, the chaos of the warlord era, the long and bitter civil war, the triumphant march of Communism — each presented Hong Kong with what a governor would later describe as its "problem of people".

When a Communist victory was assured in China in 1949, the surge of refugees reached a flood. At times more than ten thousand arrived in a week by plane, boat or train. Most, however, crossed the hills of the New Territories on foot.

There were wealthy Shanghai bankers and businessmen with plenty of money to buy them security; orphans with nothing and no one in the world, caught up in the southward-bound human current. The rich bought terraced villas on the Peak, surrounded by whispering bamboos and azaleas. The poor crowded the suffocating gloom of dingy tenements, or begged and stole the corrugated iron and packing cases necessary for shelter.

Both began to work towards a new life: the rich investing their expertise and salvaged capital in textile mills and factories; the poor labouring untold hours to secure a better life for their children.

The survival skills they evinced were already very much part of the Hong Kong psyche — and together would create what the world later dubbed an "economic miracle".

Heavy drapes, punkahs and palms provided a cool retreat for the lady of the house.

Isabella Davis, watched by her family, embarks on a sedan chair journey.

The Portuguese enjoyed an early trading advantage over other foreign merchants in China.
After helping imperial Chinese forces defeat a troublesome band of pirates disrupting coastal shipping,
China allowed the Portuguese to establish a base in Macao during the 16th century.

Source of Photographs